# TOTAL BRAIN COACHING

## A Holistic System of Effective Habit Change

For the Individual, Team, and Organization

Ted Wallace, MS, Robert Keith Wallace, PhD, Samantha Wallace

ISBN 978-0-9990558-7-8

Library of Congress Control Number 2019919395




DharmaPublications.com

**Dharma Publications, Fairfield, IA**

To Our Very Dear Children and Grandchildren

Also by Robert Keith Wallace and Samantha Wallace

THIS IS THE COMPANION BOOK TO:

## The Coherence Code

*How to Maximize Your Performance And Success in Business*
*For Individuals, Teams, and Organizations*

Robert Keith Wallace PhD, Ted Wallace, MS, Samantha Wallace

# Contents

## PART 3: LIFE

## PART 4: RESOURCE MATERIAL

# Foreword

I am extremely fortunate to have had extraordinary mentors in my life. And I would like to specifically mention those professionals who have helped me realize my vocation as an Agile coach focused on habit change.

I began this journey 15 years ago when I was the CEO of an Ayurvedic herbal supplement company. At that time I had the opportunity to learn from several top consultants, including Ankur Malek, who created RealAcad, and Steve Baumgartner, who started the Habit Change Company. What I discovered was that to improve the performance of a company you must first change the habits of the individuals.

Later, when I became an Agile coach, I realized that my main mission was to change the culture of the company I was working with. To accomplish this, I had to change the habits and mindset of the leadership, teams, and employees.

Pete Behrens, a world-renowned Agile coach, inspired me to pursue the creation of an effective system of habit change.

I learned more about Agile coaching from my remarkable teachers Cherie Silas, Michael de la Maza, and the BAYLN SIG group, and began to understand the value of transformational coaching for habit change.

My experience at Cambridge Investment Research and my interaction with its Scrum Masters, Agile coaches, and the Toastmasters club, has been significant in developing the ideas for this book.

I have made several presentations on the topic to professional groups and received support and feedback from experts in business and Agile. I would especially like to thank Pat Reed, Huy Nguyen, Gitan Shah, and Nat Goldhaber.

It has been my great good fortune to work with my father, a neurophysiologist with a deep understanding of neuroplasticity and the gut-brain axis, and with my stepmother, who is an accomplished writer.

I am always learning from my amazing wife, Danielle, and our three children, Jace, Kyran, and Myka, who had to listen to my ideas for countless hours and gave me excellent feedback. I deeply appreciate the ongoing support of my mom, brother, and two sisters.

My special thanks to George Foster for his exceptional cover design, and to Everett Day for his creativity in illustrating the symbols that represent the 7 Principles of the Coherence Code.

*Total Brain Coaching* is meant to be an instructional guide for coaches on how to improve individual, team, and organizational performance through effective holistic habit change. It is the companion book to *The Coherence Code*, a story of how a company goes from the brink of failure to success using Total Brain Coaching.

This book is not meant to be the final word on habit change. It is the beginning. We have created a non-profit organization, the

Total Brain Foundation, to foster the development of a series of protocols for habit change. All profits from this book will go to this foundation.

*Total Brain Coaching* is the start of an open source document which will ultimately produce an effective habit change methodology for the transformation, improvement, and evolution of the mindset and habits of people everywhere (see totalbraincoaching.com).

Ted Wallace

# Introduction

D oug Hatchett's cheeks are flaming as he storms into his office. "I'm the CEO, Smith can't push me aside like that," he screams. "If he doesn't appreciate my leadership I may as well quit."

Fifty-five-year-old Doug isn't always hysterical. He can be perfectly normal and agreeable for days and weeks, working hard to accomplish SMITH & HATHAWAY'S goals, until...some small thing throws him into a rage. Lately his work situation has become more stressful and his outbreaks are more frequent. Doug has called you, as a Total Brain Coach, and asked you to help him improve his situation.

This book explains the basics of Total Brain Coaching, or TBC, and shows you how to help Doug and other clients. Let's begin with a brief definition of Total Brain Coaching, and then consider its fundamental principles and tools.

Total Brain Coaching is an effective, holistic system to help individuals, teams, and businesses to change their habits. It is based on 7 guiding principles presented in the companion book, *The Coherence Code*. These principles are easy to remember using "DHARMIC" as an acronym:

## D – DISCOVER YOUR ENERGY STATE

Once an individual, team, or organization decides to make a change, they need to understand their Energy State, and how different external factors affect their inherent strengths and weaknesses.

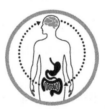

## H – HARNESS YOUR NEUROPLASTICITY
## AND GUT-BRAIN AXIS

It is easier to create a new habit than to change an old one. Habits are like neural circuits and to establish a new habit involves the creation of new wiring in the brain.

## A – USE THE POWER OF ATTENTION

The fastest and easiest way to create a new habit is to use your power of attention to initiate small doable steps.

## R – FIND YOUR INNER RHYTHM

Each individual, team, or organization has their own inner rhythm. Being in tune with their rhythm makes it easier to incorporate a new habit into pre-existing routines.

## M – USE THE FEEDBACK MATRIX

For maximum coaching results, use the Feedback Matrix, which involves four techniques: Self-Coaching, Personal Coaching, Group Coaching, and Environmental Coaching.

## I – CONTINUAL IMPROVEMENT AND INTEGRATION

Each step of progress should be measured and evaluated. Rapid feedback helps facilitate improvement and integration.

## C – CELEBRATE STEPS OF SUCCESS

Recognize small changes in habits and use positive reinforcement to celebrate every stage of achievement.

.

### Chapter Summaries

In Chapters 1 to 9 each of the above principles and tools is explained in greater detail. In Chapters 10 and 11, these concepts are applied to teams and the organizations. In Chapters 12 to 15, we consider the application of Total Brain Coaching to other areas of life.

### Chapter 1

Chapter 1 - Part A introduces the 1st tool of Total Brain Coaching, **The Energy State Quiz**. The Energy State Quiz is a key assessment tool, which helps you understand who your client is and how they can make changes in their life. In the case of Doug, this tool will help him understand why he is prone to anger issues.

Chapter 1 - Part B helps you, as the coach, understand: Why certain Energy States collide while others blend and even complement each other. This knowledge will guide your interaction with your clients, and improve their relationships at work and home.

## Chapter 2

In Chapter 2, you will learn the 2nd tool of Total Brain Coaching: **Make a Habit Map and Plan**. It turns out that it is easier to learn a new habit than to change an old one. Doug clearly needs to work on his anger issues. He has already taken anger management classes but he is still not able to keep his temper under control. You can help him decide what new habit would best allow him to eliminate this behavior.

## Chapter 3

In Chapter 3, you are introduced to the 3rd tool: **Create a New Habit**. We can think of habits as neural circuits in the brain through which information flows freely. It is difficult to disassemble these super highways, and much easier to build a new pathway. We create new habits by "harnessing" our neuroplasticity. Neuroplasticity is the ability of the brain to change itself at any moment. Because the brain is a physical organ, change takes energy and time. Total Brain Coaching will help Doug create a new habit in simple, easy steps. And because the brain is connected to the gut and other systems through the gut-brain axis, your client will not only be rewiring his brain, but he or she will also be making other beneficial changes to their entire physiology.

**Chapter 4**

In Chapter 4, you learn the 4th tool: **Focus your Power of Attention** on one habit. There are a number of ways to use the power of attention to help Doug and your other clients change their habits. Make sure your client is receptive to change and encourage them to pick a habit that suits their Energy State. Help them focus on one new habit at a time and have them make changes in small steps.

**Chapter 5**

In Chapter 5, you will learn the 5th tool: **Find your Inner Rhythm and Mobilize your Energy Resources**. Asking the right questions can enable your client to discover their inner rhythm and how they can mobilize their energy resources for habit change.

Once a client's energy level is strong enough to begin the habit change process, it is then useful to educate them on the routines that best suit their Energy State. Doug likes routines that have clear objects. You can help Doug by showing him how to piggy-back a positive new habit onto one of his existing routines.

**Chapter 6**

In Chapter 6, you will learn the 6th tool: **Use the Feedback Matrix**, which consists of four different coaching techniques—Self-coaching, Personal coaching, Group coaching, and Environmental coaching. Each of these different techniques helps to reinforce a new habit.

Self-coaching is when clients are taught how to learn and monitor new habits by themselves. The Self-coaching approach offers Doug specific things that he can do on his own, such as keeping a journal and doing self pulse (see Resource Material 4).

As your client's personal coach, your goal is to empower them to develop a plan of their own, which has specific objectives. The ultimate goal for Doug is to adopt a new habit that will keep his Energy State in balance and help him avoid triggers that might cause him to lose his temper. You can also help Doug and other clients improve their communication with friends, family, and team members, so that the result can be resonance rather than friction.

Group coaching is when the client works with a group who is also trying to form a similar positive new habit. Doug will gain valuable support by sharing his experiences, especially with those who have the same Energy State.

Environmental coaching is when the client assesses the impact of different environmental factors on his or her ability to form a new habit. Doug is likely to be more successful if he takes responsibility for making the change in his environment.

## Chapter 7

In Chapter 7, you will learn the 7th tool: **Continual Improvement and Integration**. For lasting habit change, it is essential for your client to have fast-feedback loops to reinforce their habit. Habit change is more likely to be successful when there are clear definable goals. These goals help your client become accountable.

It will be good for Doug to have a journal in which he records how many anger events he had in a week and their intensity. He can then go over the results with his coach to evaluate how he is doing and decide what he can do to improve. The learning of a new habit can sometimes feel like taking two steps forward and one step back because each time you learn something new you have to integrate it into your neural network and this takes time and energy.

**Chapter 8**

In Chapter 8, you will learn the 8th tool: Using the power of positive reinforcement by **Celebrating Steps of Success**. Both positive and negative attention can stimulate a person to change a habit. Total Brain Coaching uses the positive approaching, always encouraging and appreciating the steps of progress to create a new habit. Celebrate your client's steps of progress in creative ways at specific milestones.

**Chapter 9**

In Chapter 9 you will consider how different tools can be organized into specific **habit change systems**. One of the main goals of Total Brain Coaching is the creation of protocols for different types of coaching.

**Chapters 10 and 11**

In Chapters 10 and 11, you will understand the three basic strategies that are used in Total Brain Coaching to **change the culture of an organization**. The first approach involves evaluating the current culture and envisioning where you want it to be. It may be that it is advantageous to choose a new system of work that will reinforce the culture you want. The second involves educating and changing the mindset of the leadership. But to do that you need to also change their habits. The third and final step involves setting up a coaching and learning program that will enable all the employees and teams to change their mindset and habits.

**Chapters 12 to 15**

In Chapters 12 to 15 we consider the application of Total Brain Coaching to **other areas of life**: health coaching, relationship coaching, parent coaching, and life coaching.

# PART 1

## THE INDIVIDUAL

# CHAPTER 1: PART A

## DISCOVER YOUR ENERGY STATE

S elf-awareness is empowering. The more people learn about who they are, the more they will naturally excel, even in a demanding environment. Total Brain Coaching personalizes your client's habit change journey according to their individual Energy State. Many businesses today use tests like the Myers-Briggs Type Indicator, Kolbe, and Strength Finders, to help create a more open corporate environment by educating employees to become aware of the effect of their personality on their relationships. There is one specific tool especially effective for habit change—the Energy State Quiz of Total Brain Coaching.

### The Energy State Quiz

The Energy State Quiz is derived from the time-tested mind/ body/gut assessment used in Ayurveda, one of the most effective systems of natural health. This method has a huge advantage over all other assessment tests because it is based on the underlying psychological and physiological differences among individuals. A growing body of scientific research reveals a correlation between the three main Energy States and distinct genetic, biochemical, and physiological markers (see Resource Material 2).

Ayurveda determines how different factors influence each person's Energy State, either positively or negatively. One of the most important factors, for example, is diet, which can create either balance or imbalance in the individual's Energy State. Modern science has only recently discovered that different foods turn genes on or off. Each one of us is different and we react differently to environmental triggers. Ayurveda can be considered to be an ancient science of epigenetics, explaining how environmental factors affect our DNA without changing its basic structure.

The Energy State Quiz identifies specific environmental triggers that cause your client to go out of balance and perform poorly. By understanding your client's particular Energy State, it is much easier to help them adopt and maintain new, positive habits. It is also essential for you, as a coach, to understand your own Energy State and triggers.

Let's briefly consider the three main Energy States:

1. The V Energy State, which Ayurveda calls Vata (vah'tah), we call simply "V". V Energy State individuals can be enthusiastic and inventive creators. In business they are open and sensitive to the customer's needs, ready to explore new options, and often producing

innovative campaigns.

2. The P Energy State, which Ayurveda calls Pitta (pit′ah), we call simply "P". P Energy State people are dynamic and purposeful achievers. They are highly motivated to help employees, teams, and the entire company fulfill their specific goals.

3. The K Energy State, which Ayurveda calls Kapha (kah′fah), we call simply "K". K Energy State people are usually steady and good-natured organizers. They can make trustworthy and high performing administrators, who are able to carefully optimize procedures and business practices, increasing harmony and productivity.

There are a number of ways to assess a person's Energy State and the simplest is the quiz below, which we have adapted from the book *Dharma Parenting*. You will also find it in *Total Brain Coaching*'s companion book, *The Coherence Code*. For more detailed versions of the quiz go to doshaguru.com, dharmaparenting.com and docgut.com.

# CHAPTER 1: PART B

## INTERACTIONS BETWEEN ENERGY STATES

As a coach, it is important for you to understand the interactions between your own Energy State and that of your client or employee. The following examples include interactions between the three main Energy States.

**Situation #1: The P Coach with a P Employee or Client**

P coaches and P clients are well suited to each other and tend to enjoy a symbiotic relationship. You both love competition and have no problem with discipline. You both are goal-oriented and will probably consider the challenge of habit change to be a fun endeavor.

Advice: If either of you is out of balance, fireworks may ensue. You both want to be right and neither of you will shrink from a heated argument.

- Be sure to schedule your P coaching sessions after you have both had a meal.

• Meet in an air-conditioned room.

## Situation #2: The P Coach with a V Employee or Client

P coaches are good at structuring a routine that helps to keep a V client grounded and in balance. The routine, however, must be attractive to the creative nature of your V Client.

Advice: P coaches can be controlling and overbearing and may be willing to achieve results at any cost. This will not work with a V client. As a P coach, you must be able to empathize rather than dominate your V client. Be considerate. For instance, ask your V client if you are speaking too loudly or forcefully and really listen to their thoughts and ideas!

• If you become frustrated, do not try and correct them, even if you are right.

• "Feelings" is the operative word with a V Energy
State person.

## Situation #3: The P Coach with a K Employee or Client

P coaches and K clients can work well as a team, with one providing dynamic energy to the combination, and the other contributing stability and patience. The K client usually appreciates the energy of their P coach.

Advice: Again, the P coach needs to be in tune with the different nature of their K client. Slow down. Listen. And don't worry about how long anything takes.

• Enjoy the easygoing nature of your K client, and allow

them to come to their own conclusions in their own time.

- Remember that encouragement and a little direction will greatly benefit the K client, as long as you are not intense or pushy.

**Situation #4: The V Coach with a V Employee or Client**

Since the V coach and the V client have similar inclinations and sensitivities, they will probably enjoy each other's company. The V coach will appreciate the creativity and imagination of the V client's style as long as it doesn't meander in too many wild directions.

Advice: The V coach needs to recognize the changeable V nature of their client and help to keep them focused. If the V client becomes imbalanced due to stress or fatigue, the session will require extra skill and finesse.

- First, allow your client to talk and get everything out.

- Then gently help them focus and direct their attention to the topic at hand.

**Situation #5: The V Coach with a P Employee or Client**

This is an interesting pairing. V and P go well together, unless the P client gets out of control. The V coach must be especially careful to remain in good balance. The enthusiasm and creativity of the V can help a tightly wound up P to relax and move forward.

Advice: Listen carefully and your P client may do a lot of work for you. They love goals and a challenge, and enjoy making precise

## Energy State Quiz

The short quiz below, adapted from the book *Dharma Parenting*, gives you an idea of your Energy State.

| V ENERGY STATE | STRONGLY DISAGREE / STRONGLY AGREE | | | | |
|---|---|---|---|---|---|
| 1. Light sleeper, difficulty falling asleep | [1] | [2] | [3] | [4] | [5] |
| 2. Irregular appetite | [1] | [2] | [3] | [4] | [5] |
| 3. Learns quickly but forgets quickly | [1] | [2] | [3] | [4] | [5] |
| 4. Easily becomes overstimulated | [1] | [2] | [3] | [4] | [5] |
| 5. Does not tolerate cold weather very well | [1] | [2] | [3] | [4] | [5] |
| 6. A sprinter rather than a marathoner | [1] | [2] | [3] | [4] | [5] |
| 7. Speech is energetic, with frequent changes in topic | [1] | [2] | [3] | [4] | [5] |
| 8. Anxious and worried when under stress | [1] | [2] | [3] | [4] | [5] |
| V SCORE | *(TOTAL YOUR RESPONSES)* | | | | |

| *P ENERGY STATE* | *STRONGLY DISAGREE*  /  *STRONGLY AGREE* | | | | |
|---|---|---|---|---|---|
| 1. Easily becomes overheated | [1] | [2] | [3] | [4] | [5] |
| 2. Strong reaction when challenged | [1] | [2] | [3] | [4] | [5] |
| 3. Uncomfortable when meals are delayed | [1] | [2] | [3] | [4] | [5] |
| 4. Good at physical activity | [1] | [2] | [3] | [4] | [5] |
| 5. Strong appetite | [1] | [2] | [3] | [4] | [5] |
| 6. Good sleeper but may not need as much sleep as others | [1] | [2] | [3] | [4] | [5] |
| 7. Clear and precise speech | [1] | [2] | [3] | [4] | [5] |
| 8. Becomes irritable and/or angry under stress | [1] | [2] | [3] | [4] | [5] |
| *P SCORE* | *(TOTAL YOUR RESPONSES)* | | | | |

| K Energy State | Strongly Disagree / Strongly Agree | | | | |
|---|---|---|---|---|---|
| 1. Slow eater | [1] | [2] | [3] | [4] | [5] |
| 2. Falls asleep easily but wakes up slowly | [1] | [2] | [3] | [4] | [5] |
| 3. Steady, stable temperament | [1] | [2] | [3] | [4] | [5] |
| 4. Doesn't mind waiting to eat | [1] | [2] | [3] | [4] | [5] |
| 5. Slow to learn but rarely forgets | [1] | [2] | [3] | [4] | [5] |
| 6. Good physical strength and stamina | [1] | [2] | [3] | [4] | [5] |
| 7. Speech may be slow and thoughtful | [1] | [2] | [3] | [4] | [5] |
| 8. Possessive and stubborn under stress | [1] | [2] | [3] | [4] | [5] |
| *K Score* | *(Total your responses)* | | | | |

Compare your three scores. Whichever total is higher, V, P, or K, is your primary Energy State. It is common for people to have two high scores and one lower score. This indicates that you are a combination of two main Energy States, with a minor influence from the third one. In some cases, you may have three similar scores, which indicates that you have a Tri-Energy State.

plans and being accountable. However, you must always be prepared in case your P client goes out of balance. Do not engage. Calmly and respectfully end the session and wait for a better time to coach.

- Do not let the P client's overheated emotions overwhelm or imbalance you.

- Be well rested, centered, and prepared to stay at least one step ahead.

**Situation #6: The V Coach with a K Employee or Client**

The easygoing nature of K clients can make coaching simple, but remember as a V coach, you are operating at a very different speed than your client, and you will have to be extra patient, which is not always easy.

Advice: Above all, you must be rested. Your creative powers and imagination have to be fully charged in order for you to be able to help your client move towards positive habit change.

- Go slower!

- Maintain focus on the goal and allow your K client to share your energy and enthusiasm.

**Situation #7: The K Coach with a K Employee or Client**

K coaches and K clients are usually happy together, as long as neither is overtired. One problem may be that progress toward habit change might move at a snail's pace. Slow and steady does win the race, but how long do you want to wait?

Advice: If your K client is out of balance, extra energy will be needed on your part. If both of you are out of balance, the best thing will be to enlist outside help from a friendly P coach or knowledgeable friend.

- Keep moving!

- Create new and stimulating approaches.

**Situation # 8: The K Coach with a V Employee or Client**

This combination works well because the natural qualities of a good K coach have a grounding and supportive effect on the V client. More than any other Energy State, the K coach has the patience and stability to be able to successfully handle a changeable and emotional V client.

Advice: If you, as a K coach, go out of balance, your anxiety-prone V client will certainly suffer.

- Do whatever you have to do in order to stay well rested.

- Ensure that your energy is only positive and uplifting.

**Situation # 9: The K Coach with a P Employee or Client**

The calm K coach is capable of handling the most difficult situations. And the P client is motivated and ready for change. What could be more ideal?

Advice: If you are out of balance, it will be very hard to control your P client. Make sure that you keep your energy high and check that your P client is cool and has a snack if needed.

- Be flexible.

- Don't lose control of your intense, strong-willed P client.

Most people have a combination of Energy State, which means that there will be many variations in the interactions between coach and client.

# CHAPTER 2

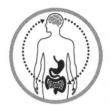

# CREATING A HABIT MAP AND PLAN

One of your jobs as a coach is to help your client create a Habit Map and Plan. Help is the key word. You help them by not giving advice, or in any way telling them what to do, but by asking empowering questions and encouraging them to come up with their own plan. This process is much easier if you know the results of your client's Energy State Quiz.

Begin by asking your client to write, in the center of a page, what they would most like to change. In Doug's case—reduce anger meltdowns. Then ask him to think of possible ways that he might accomplish this goal.

Total Brain Coaching uses two main methods: coaching and educating. The coaching mode is the more effective because it enables you to allow your client to come to his own conclusions. The problem is that he may not realize what the triggers are that cause him to be angry. Using the educating approach, you can help Doug understand that as a P Energy State individual, very specific triggers will probably cause him to become irritable. According to Ayurveda, these include:

- Not eating on time

- Becoming overheated

- Spicy food

Once Doug recognizes these triggers, it will be easier for him to identify what new habit he wants to adopt so that he can stay in balance and not lose his temper. The most important of these to control anger is not eating on time. So Doug's Habit Plan is simple: Make sure to eat lunch on time every day.

For an idea of how creating a habit plan might apply to other clients, let's consider Rob, who came to me with the desire to lose weight. His Energy State Quiz results revealed that he was a combination of a P and K Energy State, with P dominating slightly. I took him through the process of creating a Habit Map with his prime goal, losing weight, in the center. Then I asked him to think of possible ways that he might accomplish his goal and asked him to write each new idea on his map—like spokes emerging from a central hub. I explained that he could express his ideas either in the form of words, lists, or drawings (using different colors if he wanted). Once Rob's map was done, I helped him to create a Habit Plan from information listed on the map.

Rob's map included several different approaches to losing weight, from eating less to exercising more. In order to narrow down the choices, I asked him to choose the top five approaches he wanted to make. Then, I asked him to select the top three, and out of those, the top one. Rob's #1 choice was "eating less." Now we had a starting point, and we went on to consider his Energy State.

If Rob had been a V Energy State person, it would have been very easy to achieve his main goal because V individuals like to eat small amounts and weight is not a problem for them until they are older. Rob is a combination P and K Energy State and he will have a harder time. His P Energy State requires good-size meals, so eating less was going to be challenging for him. As a part K Energy person, Rob can actually skip meals. That's the good news. The bad news is that a K Energy person has a slower metabolism, which means that Rob gains weight easily.

Before Rob began his new habit of eating less, I asked him, "Where would you like to be in a year?" This started him thinking about ways that this habit change had to be integrated into his life. It's important for the client to have a clear vision of the goal. For Rob, it was the idea of losing 5 pounds over the next month (an easy and simple objective) and then maintaining that weight for at least a year. In order to create a more comprehensive life plan, it is important for your client to first experience success with one habit. When they have confidence in their ability to make one change, you can then have them decide on another habit they want to adopt.

CHAPTER 3

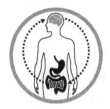

## CREATE A NEW HABIT:

HARNESSING YOUR NEUROPLASTICITY AND
GUT-BRAIN AXIS

Your brain is dynamic and it continues to change through-out your entire life. This is the result of neuroplasticity, the ability of the nervous system to form new connec-tions and pathways. Changes in the brain might be as simple as the addition of a few molecules to a nerve membrane, or as com-plex as the formation of an entirely new neural network.

At birth your brain has billions of nerve cells, but the pathways between them have not yet been formed. During your first three years of life, our brain cells create as many as twenty-four million neural connections each minute.

Early childhood is the time when your brain is most "plastic"—most adaptable. Injuries during this period are corrected with

35

surprising speed. If one area of the brain is damaged, tasks and functions can be transferred to another area. As you get older, some of this flexibility is lost, but your brain still has the potential to adapt. With appropriate rehabilitation techniques, many stroke victims, for example, are able to make a remarkable recovery.

Neuroplasticity takes many forms. From the age of three to ten, you have more connections between your brain circuits than at any other time of your life. From ten to seventeen, you lose one to two percent of these connections each year in a process called "neural pruning." Like the pruning of a shrub or tree, when some of the branches and shoots are removed, the plant becomes stronger and leaves and fruits increase. Pruning within the brain is also a way of maximizing energy and resources. The pathways that are strengthened are those which are in use, while pathways not being used are absorbed back into the brain. It's the old principle, "Use it or lose it."

## Brain Development

Brain development is not only about the number of connections between nerve cells, it also is about the types of connections. As your brain matures certain nerve fibers gain the ability to transfer information faster than others. How does this happen? Certain supportive cells in the brain surround a nerve fiber and insulate it with a fatty coating called myelin, which speeds up nerve transmission. This takes place in the important frontal part of the brain, the "executive area" for planning and decision-making.

Neurologists often give the example of teenagers who look like adults and sometimes behave like adults, but lacking fully developed connections to the frontal areas of their brain, their judgment is immature and they may make poor choices which can get them into trouble.

By the time you are 25 years old, your frontal executive brain circuits are completely mature. Does this mean that you are using the full potential of your brain? Almost certainly you are not.

Brain development is a prime example of nature vs. nurture. Our DNA is programmed to lay down certain basic pathways and for our entire lives our environment has a huge effect on the modification of these pathways. The forces of nature and nurture shape all of our behavior and habits. Children who have been abused or neglected, for example, are more likely to have poor mental and physical health, as well as an increased tendency toward substance abuse and addiction.

As we said earlier, habits can be thought of as highways in the brain, along which information flows unimpeded. The longer you have the habit, the bigger the highway becomes, and the more difficult it is to change. But new roads and highways are constantly being formed. Every time you learn a new skill, every time you have a new experience, your brain changes. This is the extraordinary gift of neuroplasticity.

### Forming a New Habit

It is much easier to form a new habit than to remove an old one.

The "use it or lose it" principle ensures that when you create a new highway in the brain and stop using the old one, that old highway will eventually become less and less prominent. It may or may not disappear completely, but it will no longer continue to dominate your behavior.

In *The Power of Habits*, Charles Duhigg talks about the three main components of a habit: cue, routine, and reward. The Golden Rule of changing a habit, according to Duhigg, is to keep the same cue and reward, but change the routine. He explains that one of the main approaches of AA, for example, is to substitute the negative routine of drinking with the positive routine of going to AA meetings. These meetings are designed to provide psychological rewards such as companionship, sharing emotions, and catharsis. This same technique of habit change has been used by other organizations and while it can work, bad habits and addictions are not easy to change.

To build and strengthen a new, more beneficial habit, you can either substitute a new routine or adopt a completely new habit. In Doug's case, he started a new habit, which might seem unrelated to his meltdown problem. The rationale for starting this new habit was based on the knowledge of his individual Energy State. I helped him to become aware of the fact that when he missed his lunch, it upset the balance of his P Energy State and resulted in irritability and anger. The simple conclusion was that by creating a new habit of eating his lunch on time he could prevent future meltdowns.

I took a different approach with Rob. He wanted to eat less, so I helped him create a new routine that allowed him to put more attention on the process of eating. Instead of gulping his food down quickly, as he had done in the past, we substituted the new routine in which he ate more slowly and was more attentive to the food.

Building a new habit requires both time and energy. One study showed that it took 20 days to establish the habit of drinking a glass of water at the beginning of the day, and it took 84 days to establish the habit of doing 50 sit-ups every day. Simple habits will take a relatively short time to establish, while more difficult habits can take substantially longer. It is important to explain this to your client so that he or she has reasonable expectations.

In Doug's case, making sure that he ate lunch on time each day wasn't very difficult. Until he took his present high-powered job, he had been used to eating his lunch on time, so it was a habit that he could easily re-establish.

In Rob's case, maintaining the new routine of putting more attention on the food will be harder because it's not something he has done before. It might be even more difficult when he goes out to eat with friends or when he travels and can not control conditions.

Every situation is different and depends on what works best for your client's individual Energy State and a changing environment. There is one thing, however, which would help both Doug and Rob—the adoption of a super habit.

### Super Habits

In his book, Duhigg describes how learning a "keystone," or

super habit, can help change other habits. He tells the story of Lisa Allen, a 34-year-old woman who was about to get a divorce. Lisa had had problems with smoking and drinking since she was sixteen.

In an attempt to experience some relief from her problems she took a vacation to Cairo. It wasn't a great vacation because she was unhappy about her relationship with her husband and worried about being in debt. Then, out of nowhere, she had the idea of returning to Egypt the following year to trek in the desert. In order to achieve this physically demanding goal, however, she realized that she would have to stop smoking. Duhigg explains that a single habit change, in this case giving up smoking, can act as a keystone habit. Once Lisa stopped smoking, she was able to give up other bad habits and create new positive habits, which dramatically improved her physical and mental health.

There are many examples of keystone habits—starting yoga, running marathons, participating in a charity, or studying art or music—all of which have helped to change peoples' lives. One of the most powerful keystone habits is meditation. And the most widely studied meditation technique is Transcendental Meditation, or TM. Research has shown that TM is effective in reducing and even eliminating numerous harmful habits, including cigarette and alcohol use and drug addiction. TM creates greater orderliness or coherence in the brain as measured by EEG coherence and it has been suggested that this increase in brain coherence is the result of the formation of a new neural network. These new brain pathways allow people to more easily change both physical and mental habits. (For more information on TM and other forms of meditation, see Resource Material 3.)

Starting TM would be an excellent choice for both Doug and Rob. For Doug, research shows that TM creates more settled emotions and helps with anger issues. For Rob, this new super habit could allow him adopt better dietary habits. According to Ayurveda, diet and digestion are not only critical for weight loss, but for all aspects of health, and modern science now recognizes the ancient concept of food as medicine.

## Your Gut-Brain Axis

One of the most important and revolutionary discoveries in modern science is the existence of the gut-brain axis and its influence on mental and physical health. The gut-brain axis consists of the nervous system, endocrine system, immune system, the special nervous system of the gut called the enteric nervous system, and perhaps most important, our gut bacteria, often referred to as the microbiome. Yes, the composition of your gut bacteria is one of the most important factors for your health.

The microbiome consists of all the microorganisms in your body, and the largest quantity of these microscopic creatures are the 30 trillion bacteria in your gut, which have the ability to influence your brain and other parts of your body. Recently published scientific papers suggest that gut bacteria may be involved in numerous diseases from auto-immune disorders to heart disease. There are even studies which show that gut bacteria can influence how stress affects your state of mind, determining whether you are happy, sad, or depressed. Psychobiotics, a new category of drugs, consists of probiotics or friendly bacteria that can help improve mental health.

Harnessing your neuroplasticity is a great tool to help you change habits. And improving your gut health will give you an even better chance. If your client changes a habit that has to do with the kind of food he or she regularly consumes, it will alter the gut bacteria and the expression of genes in their DNA. Every new habit changes your brain, your gut-brain axis, and your DNA.

You already know that it would be better for you to eat a healthier diet, but talking about it and actually doing it are separate realities. Should you follow a Paleo diet or the Mediterranean diet? There are so many choices and they often compete with each other. We are in the middle of the Diet Wars, with every doctor and health expert claiming that they have the solution to a healthier, longer life.

For Rob, eating less might not be enough for him to lose weight if he is also having digestive problems. You may have to help him learn new habits to help repair and heal his gut so that he will be able to digest his food more effectively. He might also have to reboot his microbiome in order to lose weight.

In our recent books, *Gut Crisis* and *The Rest and Repair Diet*, we offer health coaching guidelines and specific tools to help heal your client's digestion and gut health. The primary emphasis of this diet is to detox and heal the digestive tract and to reboot the microbiome.

Personalizing your client's diet and lifestyle according to his or her Energy State will improve their physical and mental health and give them more energy. It takes a lot of energy to change a habit. Total Brain Coaching provides the strategies needed to create new habits.

# CHAPTER 4

## THE POWER OF ATTENTION

I t is an ancient and world-wide understanding that the more attention you put on something, the stronger it becomes in your life. Total Brain Coaching uses the power of attention to help clients adopt new habits. As a coach, your attention is on actively listening and asking the right questions. Only then can you help your client focus their attention on the habit they want to change. As an educator, you have information about their specific Energy State that will help them. Each Energy State manifests a different type of attention.

The attention of a V Energy State person, for example, can be precise but it tends to move quickly from one topic to another. V Energy State people are more sensitive than other types and can be overwhelmed by an overload of sensory information, and also,\ by too many choices. When coaching a V Energy individual, it might be necessary for you to gently help them stay focused. You have to be subtle about it, however, because if they feel that you are pushing them, dampening their creativity, or in any way shutting them down, there may well be a strong emotional reaction. If they become excited and out of balance, it will be almost impossible for them to focus their attention.

The attention of the P Energy person is primarily on solutions and goals. These are not "stop and smell the flowers" people. They love competition and leadership and are very interested in making improvement in their own lives, so adopting a new habit will be easier for them. Time is important to a P Energy person and your communication as a coach has to be clear and to the point. You don't have to be gentle with them, but you have to earn their respect. If they are out of balance, tread lightly to avoid a blow-up.

K Energy State individuals have a very settled mindset and their attention is fixed upon regular routines. They don't like change, and you can't rush them. You must give them time to make a decision. Be patient. If they are occasionally stubborn, it probably means that they are out of balance.

If your client seems tired or stressed, their attention will be limited. Try to reschedule another coaching session at a time when they are more likely to be well-rested.

## Habit Change Plan

Doug is trying to make sure that he eats his lunch on time every day in order to prevent his anger issues. He enjoys having goals and all you need to periodically do is to give him your attention by checking in and monitoring his progress.

Rob is trying to eat less, and is trying to focus on the process of eating. When I asked him about his eating habits I learned that he was a quick eater, often finishing before anyone else, and that he sometimes ate on the run, either standing or driving, and rarely placed his full attention on his food. I asked him a series of questions, which helped him make a plan to change his eating habits merely by changing the quality of his attention. Here is what Rob and I came up with:

1. Always sit down to eat.

2. Put the fork down between bites and only pick it up again to take another bite. This may sound simplistic, but it will help Rob slow down and put more attention on his food.

3. Take time to chew and really taste the food, rather than gulping it down.

4. At the end of the meal, sit for a few minutes to help digestion, before getting up and sprinting into activity.

As a coach, you have to be careful not to tell your client what to do. At the same time, if you have information that is necessary to hear, it is okay to educate them in an easy, informative manner. You want it to be their plan and their motivation.


## Positive Attention and Appreciation

There is a YouTube video of the comedian Bob Newhart as a therapist counseling a woman client on how to stop a bad habit.

She can hardly believe it, but he insists that his technique has never failed. He first tells her that his technique is very simple and requires only two words. When at last she finishes describing her horrific phobia, Newhart leans over his desk and yells, "STOP IT!" Throughout the rest of their 5-minute session, he responds to each of her problems by repeating, "STOP IT! JUST STOP IT!" in an increasingly aggressive, commanding voice. (https://www.youtube.com/watch?v=Ow0lr63y4Mw)

If it were that easy, we would have stopped all our bad habits long ago. Negative attention may seem to work when we are young and defenseless, but it frequently leads to rebellion and the accumulation of even worse habits. Hurting your client's feelings or damaging their sense of purpose and self-esteem is clearly not the best approach. Positive attention and empathy go a long way!

Your client needs to know that you care about them. One of the fundamentals of successful coaching is to establish trust with your client. They must understand and trust that you sincerely want to help them, because only then can they be honest and open about the areas of their lives that most need help.

## Habit Change Strategies

There are a few simple strategies for adopting a new habit which have been recognized for thousands of years by traditional systems of health, such as Ayurveda and Chinese medicine, and which are now in popular habit change books like *Atomic Habits* by James Clear.

### 7 Main Steps That Involve Attention and Awareness

First, your client has to be receptive and want to change. There must be a strong desire for change. If your client is open and growth-oriented and at least believes that he or she is able to change, it will be easier for them to adopt a new habit. If your client's mindset is closed and rigid, it is much harder for them to make changes.

Second, adopt one habit at a time. When your attention is divided it becomes harder to accomplish a task. A V Energy State person may want to change several habits at once, but it is important for you to help them focus on one habit at a time. There is one exception to this rule: Adopting one keystone habit can lead to a cascade of changing habits.

Third, in the beginning, pick smaller habits to change. Ayurveda emphasizes the value of taking small steps. This approach also happens to be the main theme of the book Atomic Habits. A P Energy State person can become overly ambitious and want to make many big changes and you need to help them choose more realistic and attainable goals.

Fourth, try to have your client combine his or her new habit with similar existing habits. This is sometimes referred to as habit stacking.

Fifth, your environment makes a gigantic difference. Habit change is a lot easier if you can do it in a friendly environment. If you want to stop smoking, it makes perfect sense to choose to be around people who don't smoke. It is also very helpful to have a supporting and accountable partner who is ready to make the same habit change.

Sixth, the first habit your client wants to change should be one that is complementary to his or her Energy State. If the client is a P Energy State person, it will be better for them to choose something they can be enthusiastic about, such as "exercising more." P Energy State individuals enjoy physical activity and love a challenge. Encourage them to join a gym with other people who have the same goals.

Seventh, help your client to enjoy mastering new habits. Once he or she has adopted a new habit, take time to recognize and appreciate what they have achieved. Use their new confidence and positive energy to then go further. Help them look at the big picture and reach high to create a more meaningful life.

## CHAPTER 5

## FINDING YOUR INNER RHYTHM

T otal Brain Coaching is about helping your client get in tune with their inner rhythm and synchronizing it with the biorhythms of nature. Each of us has a particular rhythm and sense of time, depending on our individual Energy State. Often we express our inner rhythms in the kinds of routines we adopt. As a Total Brain Coach, you can help your clients' change their habits by understanding their inner rhythms and encouraging them to add new, more positive habits to their existing routines.

- V Energy State people have a very quick inner rhythm. Because it is their nature to enjoy change and crave variation in everything they do, it is hard for them to stick to any particular routine. They need all your enthusiasm and perseverance as a coach to help them keep grounded and focused. If they go off their program (and they will), you will probably have to help to calm their anxieties about

starting over again. Help them to create supportive and enjoyable routines which nourish, please, and support them.

- The P Energy State is very different. They have a medi-
  um-speed inner rhythm but it is much stronger and more
  purposeful. They have no trouble following a new routine
  as long they see that it will help to accomplish their goals.
  If they think that it doesn't benefit their path of action,
  they will almost certainly ditch it and move to a different
  routine. As a coach, you need to align your client's habit
  change program with their goals. If your P client goes off
  the program, use their competitive nature to encourage
  them to reboot.

- The K Energy State person, on the other hand, has a much
  steadier and slower inner rhythm than either V or P individuals. K Energy State people enjoy and feel nourished
  and protected by a fixed routine. Changes can be very
  difficult for them. You have to give them time to adjust and
  keep encouraging them to follow the new plan. They will
  naturally resist, preferring their fixed ways, and you need
  great patience as well as enthusiasm to help them reach
  their goals.

Doug is a P Energy person so he likes routines and will have no
trouble incorporating his new habit of eating on time. If he goes
out of balance at any time, you will need to help him stabilize and
again refocus on the goal.

Rob is a combination P and K Energy State person with two

opposite types of rhythms going on. As his coach, you can help him understand his dual nature. If his Energy States are in good balance, the different sides of his nature won't be a problem. He will focus on the goal and include the new habit into his routine in a relaxed and steady manner. If your client is V Energy person, then adopting a new habit may be easy at first and more difficult later because they really don't like to follow routines and they really do have problems sticking to them.

## Understanding Biorhythms

Ayurveda and other traditional systems of health have long understood the significance of biorhythms and routines and their importance to health. This understanding is now recognized by modern medicine, and in 2017 the Nobel Prize in Physiology and Medicine was awarded for research on the genetic basis of biological rhythms. From bacteria to humans, almost all forms of life have an internal "biological clock," which maintains an approximately 24-hour rhythm. When unnatural external signals of light and dark are introduced, your master clock becomes confused and this can create health problems. Shift workers, for instance, are shown to have a higher incidence of cancer, cardiovascular disease, digestive disorders, and obesity, as well as psychiatric and neurodegenerative diseases.

Your gut bacteria also have their own biological rhythms. When researchers transferred the gut bacteria from jet-lagged mice into germ-free mice, the recipient mice developed both glucose intolerance and obesity. Recent research on the gut bacteria reveals not only the presence of a daily rhythm, but also seasonal biorhythms—which, again, correlates with the ancient knowledge of Ayurveda.

## Adjusting Routines

Biorhythms are important for both Doug and Rob. Doug's main habit change to avoid getting "hangry" is eating lunch on time. Sometimes, however, this is impossible at work since it's common practice to skip meals when emergencies arise.

One of the key recommendations in Ayurveda is to eat your main meal at noon and have a lighter meal for dinner. This is a problem for Rob. He often skips lunch and comes home to help his wife cook a big dinner. Not eating on time doesn't affect his emotions as much as Doug's since Rob is a part K Energy State person. But eating a large meal at dinner will definitely not help him lose weight.

I asked Rob to think about how he might try to switch his main meal from dinner to lunch and he made a plan. His first step was to take advantage of the weekend to eat his main meal at lunch, and have a lighter dinner. During the following week, he made further progress. For at least one day, he made sure that he took the time during work hours to eat lunch as his main meal.

## Mobilizing Your Energy Resources

Your clients need all the resources they can access in order to rewire their brain and reboot their gut-brain axis. If they are fatigued and out of balance, their neuroplasticity will not be dynamic and they will have a more difficult time adopt new habits.

In preparation for any habit change, there are a few basic lifestyle tips that will help your client mobilize his or her energy resources and get in tune with their inner rhythm.

## Sleep

Make sure that your client gets enough sleep. Sleep is critical for clearing away toxins that build up in the brain during the day. Numerous studies have correlated lack of sleep with poor mental performance and health problems. The quantity of sleep needed depends on many factors, one of the most important of which is your client's individual Energy State.

### V Energy State

A V person often has a hard time going to sleep and is susceptible to insomnia. Help them understand that they must take extra care to avoid stimulation before bedtime and do something to relax, like taking a warm bath, listening to peaceful music, and using calming aromatherapy.

### P Energy State

A P person usually goes to sleep quickly and needs less sleep than a V. When the P is imbalanced, however, he or she may have difficulty sleeping.

## K Energy State

K energy individuals have no trouble falling asleep but they can have a hard time getting up in the morning.

## Diet and Digestion

We have already talked about the importance of the gut-brain axis and its impact on energy and mental health. Improving digestion and eating the food that is most suitable for your client's Energy State and will help keep them in good balance.

## V Energy State

V people have both a variable appetite and digestive power, which is strong at one moment and weak at another. If you are a V, you are likely to be a "snacker," who actually benefits from eating several small but nutritious meals throughout the day. Please note that it is important for a V to eat in a quiet environment, away from stress or distractions. When the V Gut is balanced, digestion is good. When the V Gut is out of balance, the individual may experience symptoms such as constipation, indigestion, and gas.

## P Energy State

The defining characteristic of the P Energy State is a powerful digestive fire. The P Gut is programmed to naturally produce a strong appetite, which needs to be satisfied at particular times during the day. As we have said, the digestive power is strongest at noon, so it's very important for P Energy individuals to eat their largest and heaviest meal at that time. When the P Gut is balanced, digestion is highly efficient; when it is out of balance, the person may experience hyperacidity, among other symptoms.

## K Energy State

K Energy State individuals have a steady digestion and can miss a meal and be without any problems. Your K Energy State client usually loves food but needs to eat only moderate amounts because they have a slower metabolism and gain weight easily. Of the three main types, Ks tend to drink the least amount of water.

For details about specific dietary recommendations for each Ayurvedic type, see *The Rest And Repair Diet: Heal Your Gut, Improve Your Physical and Mental Health, and Lose Weight.*

## Exercise

Modern medicine recognizes the value of regular exercise and scientific studies validate its many benefits. Most of us spend too much time sitting and not enough moving and stretching. One of the most popular and easiest forms of exercise is yoga (see Recommendations).

## V Energy State

V individuals are attracted to exercise that involves moving quickly but they are not suited for endurance sports. They are sprinters rather than marathoners, and must be careful not to get overtired. Activities like dancing, paddle boarding, yoga—anything that keeps them moving easily—will be good for them. V Energy State people do well with moderate, grounding, and warming workout.

**P Energy State**

P Energy State individuals are almost always extremely competitive and don't hold back. They have good stamina and strength, and are often drawn to organized sports. They are so goal-oriented that they will easily overdo exercise and pay the consequences later. P Energy State people need to avoid becoming overheated. Active water sports like swimming, surfing, and parasailing are ideal.

**K Energy State**

K Energy State individuals generally have good endurance and strength, but they need regular, active, physical exercise to keep them from becoming lethargic and overweight. Running, jogging, and an energetic gym workout are all beneficial.

## Daily Routine

A good daily routine helps to incorporate the right kind of exercise, diet, and sleep habits into your client's life in an easy and effortless manner. Stress management is an important addition to everyone's daily routine. All of the Energy States benefit greatly from the practice of meditation in the morning and early evening to clear their mind, reduce stress, and boost energy (for details about different types of meditation and their benefits see Recommendations).

# CHAPTER 6

# THE FEEDBACK MATRIX

The Feedback Matrix is a tool that includes 4 different approaches to coaching:

1. Self-coaching
2. Personal coaching
3. Group coaching
4. Environment coaching

These four approaches provide feedback to reinforce any new habit you are trying to create. It is important to note that coaching is not the same as mentoring or therapy. We don't advise clients on their skills or profession, or attempt to resolve deep-seated psychological problems. These are jobs for professionals with specific training to deal with such issues. Your job is to help your clients change their habits using a simple and effective set of tools and procedures.

## Self-Coaching

Self-Coaching is something everyone does whether we are aware of it or not. But there are tools that can help the process. Keeping a journal or using an app can be helpful. In Rob's situation, a journal is essential to help him monitor his progress since he needs to keep track of the different approaches he is using to eat less: Did he sit at lunch? Did he put his fork down after each bite? Did eating slowly help him to feel more balanced? One tool he can use to monitor the balance of his Energy State is self pulse diagnosis, which we talk about in Resource Material 4.

## Personal Coaching

Personal Coaching is one of your jobs. Sometimes people have recourse to a partner or a friend, but it's almost always better to use a professional coach. The process of change can be delicate, especially in the beginning, and requires a trained expert.

As a personal coach, you will use transformational coaching techniques to help identify what goals and milestones your client wants to achieve. There is, of course, a difference between transformation coaching and transactional coaching. Transformational coaching focuses on the person, while transactional coaching techniques focus on action and performance, such as the improvement of a particular skill.

In transformational coaching, the client generally has an issue or goal they want to resolve. The coach helps them figure out how to get there by active listening and asking powerful open-ended questions to stimulate insight and understanding. When your client speaks, you, as the coach, reflect back to them. This doesn't mean paraphrasing what your client said. It means that you tell them in your own words what you heard them say.

When I first coached Rob, I gave him an idea of what was going to happen in the coaching sessions beforehand, and we established a code of conduct. I explained that my goal was for him to find a solution and that I was there to help. At the beginning of every coaching session I asked the question, "What do you want to achieve by the end of our 45-minute session today?" The purpose of this question is to allow your client to guide his or her own journey.

Let's assume that Rob can only afford to meet once a week for six months. In principle, that should be enough time for him to accomplish measureable changes. But if, for some reason, he goes back to his old habits and starts to gain weight, you need to encourage him to not worry about temporary setbacks. Ask if his wife or a buddy could regularly check on his progress. His old neural pathways have not yet disappeared entirely and it takes only a small trigger, perhaps when he is tired or run down, to cause him to revert to a familiar bad habit, like eating too fast. Changing a habit usually requires time, energy, and also outside help.

## Group Coaching

Group Coaching may be in person or online. In both situations, it can be very reinforcing for your client to be part of a group so that he or she can see how others are coping with the challenges of sticking with a new habit! As Rob's coach, it would be helpful to put him together with a P Energy State group, in which he can interact with similar goal-oriented individuals. A compatible group can be a useful reinforcement for habit change.

## Environmental Coaching

Environmental Coaching helps your client deal with the triggers that are affecting his or her ability to make changes. In the book *Triggers*, Marshal Goldsmith emphasizes that our reactions are responses to specific situations. In Rob's case, he might be able to eating less if he removes any special treats or snacks from his home. We would like to be independent of our environment but sometimes it's hard when confronted by a particular temptation. Goldsmith uses a series of active questions to help us take responsibility and change our behavior. These active questions are discussed in the next chapter.

CHAPTER 7

# CONTINUOUS IMPROVEMENT
# AND INTEGRATION

Total Brain Coaching is a process of continual improvement and integration. It's about receiving constant feedback and helping your client move ahead at the best pace he or she can manage. Bringing your client's attention to improvements provides feedback on his or her progress and reinforces the new habit. Feedback can come from a number of sources, including the four different types of coaching programs we discussed above and the use of active questions.

## Active Questions

What is the difference between an active questions and a passive one? The passive approach is: How are you doing with your new habit today? Too often, Goldsmith explains, clients blame the environment, suggesting that their boss didn't give them time, or that there were too many distractions at work. The active approach is: Did you do your best to maintain your new habit today? This places the emphasis on the client rather than blaming others or the situation they are in. This is the heart of transformational coaching, empowering the client to take responsibility for their actions.

## Ownership of the Journey

Motivation really is everything. Your steady support and encouragement is important to help your client continuously improve. As the coach, you must help the client take ownership of his or her personal journey because this will result in the greatest chance of long-term success. We mentioned that in self-coaching it is good to keep a journal. The journal is also valuable for keeping track of information learned in the various different coaching experiences. You want to empower your client to take responsibility for integrating new information that allows them to continuously update their habit plan.

Clients need to discover for themselves what is working and what is not. If you allow them to be empowered, they will be more accountable. As a coach, you want your clients to be as self-sufficient as possible and avoid a dependent attachment relationship. If their motivation comes from within, the chances are far greater that they will follow through with their habit change plan.

Your clients may decide to give up and quit at some point. Be easy with them and encourage them to start again. A reboot is a good thing. Every time Doug restarts or reboots his plan, he needs your help, not only to re-motivate himself, but also to develop new strategies that take into account the different stimuli and temptations in the environment which are sabotaging his habit plan.

## Measuring Outcomes

A critical part of a habit change plan is having measureable outcomes. It's hard to determine success if it can't be measured. From the beginning, it is good to come to an agreement with your client on how their progress will be measured.

In Doug's case, his journal will record how many anger issues he experiences in a week. As his coach, you will help him set realistic goals. In the beginning this might mean reducing his anger outbursts to once or twice a week.

For Rob, the process is simple. By weighing himself every week, he can see if his program of eating less is working. He can also make entries in his journal describing how he feels as a result of changing his eating habits. For example, he can ask himself: How did I feel right after I ate? Did I have more energy? How was my sleep? Did I feel better the next day? If he has not lost any weight, then his main goal is not being successfully addressed and you need to help him make a new habit plan.

## Continuous Learning and Development

Continuous improvement means continuous learning and

development. Training and education is at the core of the evolution of the culture of any company. As a Total Brain Coach, you play a key role in developing all aspects of the mind and body of a company's employees and leaders in the face of ever-increasing challenges and demands.

# CHAPTER 8

## CELEBRATE THE STEPS OF SUCCESS

E veryone enjoys success and congratulations, no matter how small. As a coach, you want to give positive feedback whenever possible. It can be as simple as helping your client decide how to celebrate each step of their progress. Once Rob lost 5 pounds, he came up with the idea of taking his wife out for a special dinner or a weekend getaway to celebrate. Encouraging your clients to choose the celebration will help to keep them empowered. You want to motivate them by creating periodic milestones of their success, perhaps at one week, one month, one year. Celebrate every small win with your client.

### The Progress Principle

Researchers at Harvard examined what motivates workers to produce the greatest creative output. They studied 238 individuals from 7 companies and analyzed 12,000 diary entries to determine the key factors. What they found was that the old motivators of fear and pressure were not associated with higher performance— happiness and inner positive emotions were.

The researchers called their conclusion "the progress principle." Any type of progress experienced by the workers, either as individuals or a team, resulted in what they called a "best day" performance. Progress was also associated with positive emotions. The achievement of any sort of meaningful progress on one day led to a positive experience and resulted in increased performance the following day.

There were two other important factors for better performance. The first factor was referred to as a "catalyst," which meant any kind of support for a person or group. The second factor was any event in which they were shown respect or encouragement, and was called a "nourisher."

This study shows us the value of positive reinforcement to enhance motivation. This can be applied to many areas of life and especially habit change. You want to utilize every possible tool to keep your client motivated. Celebrating their progress is one of the most important.

## The Dopamine Feedback Loop

Let's briefly look at the brain mechanism that underlies the experience of the anticipation of reward and how it drives both good and bad habits. The psychological and physiological basis of addiction is often referred to as the dopamine feedback loop.

Produced in various parts of your brain, dopamine is a neurotransmitter which is involved in all types of behavior, including motivation. It used to be that dopamine was thought of as the "pleasure" chemical of the brain. Now, however, it is associated with the anticipation or craving of pleasure. Dopamine causes you to seek experiences that you believe will make you happy.

Many psychologists suggest that dopamine is the basis of all types of addictions from drugs to social media. Every time you smoke a cigarette, play a video game, or post a selfie, you are feeding the dopamine circuit in your brain but never fully satisfying it.

Dopamine is all about anticipating reward. When you encounter a habit cue or trigger, it causes you to anticipate a reward of some kind and your dopamine begins to flow. It is interesting that the areas in the brain dedicated to anticipation are larger than those which have to do with actual pleasure.

Feedback is critical. But when we are addicted to something unhealthy, the pleasure feedback can lead to a negative result. Total Brain Coaching is not about trying to eliminate old negative habits, but replacing them with new positive habits. The dopamine feedback loop has the power to provide the motivation that will enable a new positive habit to be maintained and permanently established.

Celebrating helps reinforce the positive feedback loop, which in turn increases your client's motivation and self-confidence. Changing one habit is only the beginning. Small wins lead to big wins. Once your client improves one part of their lives, they will inevitably want to adopt other positive habits. Each step of this process will benefit from your guidance and positive reinforcement.

# CHAPTER 9

## Protocols

E ach of these 7 principles of the Coherence Code has a number of potential tools that can be organized into specific habit change systems. One of the main aspects of Total Brain Coaching is the creation of protocols for different types of coaching. As we mentioned in the Forward, we are creating an open source document at totalbraincoaching.com, and we invite coaches to contribute their own tools and protocols.

The tools, which are part of our protocol for individual habit change, are in bold under each of the 7 principles. You will see that we include a few tools from other experts in habit change (not in bold). Under some of the tools we give examples of how the tool can be used.

See a sample protocol of personal coaching below.

## D – DISCOVER YOUR ENERGY STATE

- **Take the Energy State Quiz**

    - Educate your client about the characteristics of their Energy State

    - Identify triggers that can cause your client's Energy State to go out of balance

  - Use other assessment tools: Myers-Briggs, Strength Finders, Kolbe

## H - HARNESS YOUR NEUROPLASTICITY

## AND GUT-BRAIN AXIS

- **Create a Habit Map and Plan**

    - Make a Habit Plan prioritizing your clients main approaches

- **Create a new habit and outline the details for habit change**

  - Use Duhigg's system of habit change

## A – USE THE POWER OF ATTENTION

- **Focus your Attention on One Habit**

  - Make sure your client is receptive

  - Add a new habit to an existing old one

  - Change your client's environment to help habit change

  - Pick a new habit that is suited to your client's Energy State

- Use Clear's system of atomic habits by starting with a small change

## R – FIND YOUR INNER RHYTHM

- **Mobilize Your Energy Resources**

  - Change your client's diet and digestive habits

  - Improve your client's exercise program

  - Develop good sleep habits

  - Adopt an effective stress management system

  - Be aware of the importance of biorhythms

## M – USE THE FEEDBACK MATRIX

- **Reinforce habits**

  - Self-Coaching

  - Personal Coaching

  - Group Coaching

  - Environment Coaching

## I – CONTINUAL IMPROVEMENT AND INTEGRATION

- **Empower your client to own the process of habit change**

  - Have measurable outcomes

  - Active questions

- Use concepts from Goldsmith's book *Triggers*

## C – CELEBRATE STEPS OF SUCCESS

- **Using the power of positive reinforcement by celebrating**

  - Reward your client's milestone of progress

- Special meals

- Weekend retreats

- Celebrate small wins to create big wins

- Gamification

# PART 2

## THE TEAM AND ORGANIZATION

# CHAPTER 10

# CHANGING THE ORGANIZATIONAL CULTURE

Total Brain Coaching changes an organizational culture by developing and reinforcing the habits and mindset that will best support the mission and objectives of the group.

### Three Main Strategies

There are 3 main strategies. First, we work with the leadership of the organization to evaluate their current culture and management system and decide what changes are needed in order to achieve their objectives. Depending on the size of the company, a system change can be a challenging process and Total Brain Coaching is an invaluable tool to help make the transformation. For example, if a company wants to be more customer-centric and able to respond faster to change, they can choose Agile with a Scrum methodology (see below). To become Agile requires a change in mindset and habits which are more easily accomplished by using Total Brain Coaching at all levels—individual, team, and organization.

The second strategy is to educate the leadership and top-level managers in the fundamental principles of the new system and how it will reinforce positive new habits through feedback. You need complete cooperation and commitment from the highest levels of leadership in order to initiate and sustain progress in organizational development and evolution. Whatever system is chosen, Total Brain Coaching offers the guidance and training necessary for leaders and managers to ensure real change.

The third strategy is to align the goals of the individual employee with the goals of the team and the organization. This process takes time and requires adequate resources. It is greatly facilitated by using Total Brain Coaching to help change the habits and mindset at all levels of the organization.

## Adopting a New System and Mindset

Every few years a new management system book comes out. Why? Because the world is constantly evolving and changing and leadership is always looking for ways to improve individual and team performance to enable the company to be more successful in the current environment.

One example is Agile, a new management system and mindset that uses specific frameworks, such as Scrum, Extreme Programming, and Kanban, to improve software development by creating fast feedback loops that focus on the customer. The 5 largest companies in the world—Amazon, Apple, Facebook, Microsoft, and Google—all use Agile-like principles and practices, although they have their own names for the specific systems they use, such as "the Google Way." A number of smaller companies are also using Agile and Scrum: Airbnb, Etsy, Lyft, John Deere, Menlo Innovations, Saab, Samsung, Spotify, Tesla, Uber, and Warby Parker. Agile is now being applied beyond software development to management.

Total Brain Coaching enhances Agile by helping to change and reinforce the underlying mindset and habits of the individual, team, and organization.

## Educating Leadership

If the leaders of an organization are not educated and committed to the new system, it will be very difficult to successfully implement. If the leadership is modeling one type of behavior and mindset while they are asking the rest of the company to adopt something different, it will not reinforce the change. How do you go about educating the leaders of a company?

Even the most inspiring interactive workshops and seminars are not enough. You need to change the mindset of the leaders. But in order to be able to change their mindset, you have to change their habits. A leader might want to have an Agile mindset, but if he or she is tired and stressed they will revert to their old habits. Total Brain Coaching helps them become Agile by creating new habits which give them more energy and greater flexibility so that they can build and reinforce the new mindset. Leaders and managers become more effective by empowering their employees to improve their mindset and habits.

**Aligning the Goals of the Individual, Team, and Organization**

To transform a large company to a new system like Agile takes strong commitment and resources from all levels of the organization. It is essential to have continuous feedback so that you can determine if each part of the company is aligned and working smoothly together.

Sometimes the system you adopt has built-in tools that include coaching for individuals and teams. Agile, for example, has Scrum, which offers highly effective teamwork tools to improve performance. Problems arise if one part of an organization, for instance, the software division, becomes Agile, while another part of the company, such as operations, does not.

Total Brain Coaching helps the process of change by aligning the underlying goals of individuals and teams in all parts of the organization. One team member, for example, may want to learn a new programming language as his or her individual goal. And you might be aware that one of the team's goals is to encourage members to become more cross-functional in their programming skills. This is an ideal situation in which the goals of both the individual and the team are aligned and support the new training program.

**Changing a Team Habit**

I once met with a Production Support Department that was starting to use Scrum and asked, What are your goals for the next year? What are the biggest blockers of those goals? It turned out that their project work was constantly being interrupted by production demands.

I explained how Total Brain Coaching could help them better achieve their goals by adopting more productive habits. Based on our meetings, the head of the department decided to try it out. When I used the Energy State Quiz and found that the team was made up of mostly P Energy State individuals, I designated the team as a "P Energy" type or process-driven team.

I then helped them to create a Habit Map and Plan. The most important habit the team chose to change was "reduce multitasking." What they meant by this was that they wanted to have more time to focus on their own specific objectives, rather than multitasking, by helping other teams or departments to achieve completely different objectives.

We measured the amount of multitasking they were doing, and then focused on reducing it by creating a new habit. The team decided that they wanted to reduce multitasking by decreasing unplanned "walk-ups" from other teams. (A walk-up is when people ask for advice from a different team with different goals.) We determined that our new habit would be to refer all walk-up requests directly to the Scrum Master.

I employed all of the four types of Total Brain Coaching (self-coaching, personal coaching, group coaching, and environmental coaching) to help team members create this new habit. In the self-coaching sessions, each member of the team decided to keep track of the number of times someone came to them with a walk-up request.

During personal coaching, I worked with each individual in the team and coached them on how to minimize walk-ups by immediately referring the problem to the Scrum Master.

In my group coaching, the team met together as a group and discussed other strategies to stop walk-ups. Team members were encouraged to remind each other to refer walk-ups to the Scrum Master.

In regard to environmental coaching, I spoke with other Scrum Masters and teams and asked them to also go directly to the Scrum Master for any requests.

Multitasking time was reduced by 20% and team performance greatly improved. We decided together on a team goal to reduce walk-ups by 25% and celebrated by going out for a team lunch.

Once you begin the process of changing habits in one team, you can set up a training program to repeat this process for the other teams in the organization. Change has to begin with each individual, and then each team, and finally the organization as a whole.

### The Coherence Code

We give an example of organizational change in *Total Brain Coaching*'s companion book, *The Coherence Code*, which is a story of the transformation of a business from failure to success.

J.P. Smith, the retired founder of SMITH & HATHAWAY, has recently learned that his company is in trouble. He hopes to improve the situation by acquiring cutting-edge sports technology, which will significantly upgrade his business. A competing company, however, has seriously outbid him. To make matters worse, he receives a report from a top consulting firm which reveals numerous internal problems within SMITH & HATHAWAY, including the fact that his employees are dissatisfied and won't even recommend the company's own products.

All is not lost, however, and help comes in the form of an extraordinary world-class consultant, Dame Georgina St. George. An expert in Total Brain Coaching, her methods are unconventional. Dame Georgina likes to use samurai warriors, super athletes, and outstanding business leaders to illustrate and explain the 7 principles of the Coherence Code.

SMITH & HATHAWAY begins its evolutional journey as Dame Georgina teaches Smith the art of Total Brain Coaching. He learns about the best new management systems and adopts Agile and Scrum, which are initially incorporated into the software division. Total Brain Coaching Workshops are offered throughout the company in order to align the goals of its employees and teams with SMITH & HATHAWAY's core mission. A remarkable change begins with a transformation in the mindset and habits of the leadership, resulting in improved performance and success throughout the organization.

# CHAPTER 11

## LEADERSHIP COACHING

L eadership or executive coaching helps high potential managers to clarify their goals and improve their management style. It often involves changing certain aspects of their mindset and behavior which have limited their career path.

Total Brain Coaching (TBC) leadership coaching provides a simple, reliable way to unleash the potential of such managers and help them become more effective leaders and change-makers in their profession. Each leader has to learn what style of leadership works best for his or her individual Energy State. No one style is necessarily more effective than another.

Your role as a TBC leadership coach is to help individual executives gain a more intimate and accurate vision of who they are. Self-awareness is an important starting point for change. Once the leader really understands who he or she is, it becomes easier to align their goals with the goals of the company.

Everyone has certain strengths and weakness. Behavior is based on how your brain is wired. If brain circuits have been formed by bad habits, you need to help your clients create new pathways that will improve their behavior and create more constructive relationships. Your job is to empower them to make a habit change plan and periodically check in with them. They also need to commit themselves to the time required to rewire their brains and change their habits.

# PART 3

## LIFE

# CHAPTER 12

## HEALTH COACHING

The current profession of health coaching ranges from helping to support patients in conventional hospitals, to working in an alternative wellness health setting with clients who are more interested in natural and traditional health care.

TBC health coaches use a unique, integrative approach that combines the time-tested knowledge of Ayurveda along with the latest scientific research in modern medicine. As a TBC health coach, you will help your clients create positive health habits, while educating them about the most effective personalized preventive programs.

TBC health coaching begins by establishing trust with your client. You will then help your client identify realistic, healthy goals in areas such as diet, exercise, sleep, and stress management. Everyone is different. Using the Energy State assessment tool will greatly help your client.

One of the most important new areas in health is the understanding of the gut-brain axis and its impact on all aspects of mental and physical well being. TBC health coaching provides you with the latest knowledge and how it relates to each Energy State.

To gain a more profound understanding of Ayurveda and Integrative Medicine, it is ideal for TBC health coaches to take the Master's degree program in Maharishi AyurVeda and Integrative Medicine at Maharishi International University, an accredited university. One unique feature of this program is advanced training in Ayurveda pulse diagnosis (see Resource Materials 4).

# CHAPTER 13

## RELATIONSHIP COACHING

T BC relationship coaching helps your client to become a more empathetic and compatible partner. As a TBC relationship coach, you will be able to help your client change his or her habits and set realizable goals for a loving and harmonious relationship.

In order to have a meaningful relationship, your client must understand Energy States and how they interact. This knowledge will give them the necessary understanding of common triggers which lead to misunderstandings and blow-ups. In Chapter 1 Part B we talked about some of the possible interactions that can occur between the Energy States of a coach and a client. The examples below are specific to the relationships between personal partners.

As a TBC coach, you will learn to be aware of the nature of these interactions, and have the tools necessary to improve the relationship.

### V Partner / V Partner

When a balanced V Energy State person has a relationship with another balanced V partner, they are likely to be highly compatible and enjoy each other's creativity. Since they are both extremely sensitive, however, if one of them goes out of balance, any slight misunderstanding can cause hurt feelings. If both of these V Energy State partners go out of balance, their life may become an emotional tornado.

Advice: Both V partners need to stay grounded. V Energy State individuals dislike routines, but the right routine will help to stabilize their physiology and emotions. V Energy State people do not do well in cold and wind and must avoid them as much as possible. (At the very least they need to bundle up well in such conditions.) Sipping hot water throughout the day is a simple but powerful way to help balance V Energy and help to prevent illness. Daily warm oil self-massage with the appropriate balancing oil will also help. The master tool for inner and outer balance, is of course, meditation.

### P Partner / P Partner

Two P Energy State partners equals fire X 2! This potentially combustible combination actually works very well when they are both in good balance because they both have a lot of energy and are highly motivated. They also love competition, physical exercise, and challenges.

Advice: It is critically important that neither partner misses a meal or becomes overheated! If either of them goes out of balance, arguments and a power struggle will surely follow. Both of them need to understand exactly what triggers a P Energy State outburst. Prevention is key.

## K Partner /K Partner

K Energy State partners are like two content teddy bears. Being on time is never an issue between them because they have the same slow, steady inner rhythm. If either of one of them goes out of balance, however, stubbornness and depression may seriously strain the relationship.

Advice: They need to get out, get energized, and interact socially. This prescription includes a daily dose of active exercise. If both Ks go out of balance, they may need outside help from a coach or trusted friend.

## V Partner / P Partner

This can be an amazing relationship. The P Energy State partner is powerful, highly energetic, and driven. The V Energy State partner is sensitive, responsive, and artistic. The hot fiery P partner is complemented by the cool airy V partner. But when the P person goes out of balance, his or her internal fire goes out of control and can damage the feelings of the vulnerable V person. When they both go out of balance, the relationship can become an emotionally destructive inferno.

Advice: In this relationship especially, both partners must commit to staying in good balance. Even then, the P partner has to be careful not to be too overbearing or controlling. And the V partner has to be careful not to be too overly sensitive and reactive.

## V Partner / K Partner

This pair of opposites often makes for an ideal relationship. The calm, easygoing nature of the K partner enjoys and balances the volatile, talkative V partner. When they both are in good balance, their different operating speeds don't matter. If, however, either of them goes out of balance, their differences can suddenly cause an argument over even small things.

Advice: The V partner is the more sensitive so the K partner has to help the V remain well rested and on a good routine. If the K partner goes out of balance, then the V partner will have to muster his or her energy and strength to help their K partner get back on track. It's much much easier for both of them to take preventive steps to make sure they both stay in balance!

## P Partner / K Partner

When they are in balance the P partner is always motivated towards action and enjoys the challenges of life, while the K partner is calm and capable of handling even the most difficult situations. It is an excellent combination until either one goes out of balance and the situation falls apart. The P partner will very quickly become intense and controlling, and probably lose his or her temper. The K imbalanced partner may become withdrawn and stubborn, and therefore difficult to communicate with.

Advice: The P partner must use some of his or her great energy to help the K partner stay active and in good balance. The K partner must use his or her natural kindness and steady nature to make sure that the P partner eats on time and stays cool!

# CHAPTER 14

# PARENT COACHING

### Creating Ideal Habits

TBC parent coaching is designed to help parents improve their own habits and teaches them how to help their children to also form good habits. The tools of TBC parent coaching can be found in the book Dharma Parenting. The word "dharma" is used in this context to mean a way of living that maintains balance, supports both prosperity and spiritual values, and unfolds the highest path of individual development. The TBC parenting tools make it easier to resolve problems in the deeply rewarding but challenging world of parenthood.

As a TBC parent coach, you will help parents understand why one child learns quickly and forgets quickly, while another learns slowly and forgets slowly; why one child is hyperactive and another slow; why one falls asleep quickly but wakes in the night and another takes hours to fall asleep. Total Brain Coaching gives parents the tools they need to help unfold the full potential of their child's brain and nurture their inherent brilliance and goodness.

The first tool of TBC parent coaching is to determine their children's Energy State and identify factors that can cause it to go out of balance. Of course, it is also important to determine the Energy State of the parent and help them to stay in balance so they can avoid obvious conflicts with their children. The following is adapted from the book *Dharma Parenting*:

## The V or Vata Parent

As a V Energy State parent, your strengths are your creativity, flexibility, and your lightheartedness. When a problem arises, you can usually figure out several possible solutions to choose from. Your kids love how you sometimes whisk them off on spur-of-the-moment adventures. But V parents don't always have enough stamina for the intense 24/7 focus and resolve that parenting requires. You may find that your V mind is going in a million directions at once, your anxiety is peaking, and your energy level is dropping fast. This is why you, more than any other brain/body or Energy type, need to figure out how you can take a break to settle your wild V physiology down, and generally re-energize and regroup. Maybe you can arrange for everyone in the house to take a period of quiet time, with Vata aromatherapy, soothing music, and comfy cushions to lie around on. And if you have learned Transcendental Meditation, take twenty minutes to do it twice a day, even if you have to wait until everyone else is in bed. TM is your most powerful tool to keep your V balanced so you can be at your best.

## The P or Pitta Parent

As a P Energy State parent, your strengths are your physical energy, warmth, organizational ability, and intelligence. Your lively intellect can stimulate your children's curiosity about the world, and your warm heart and sense of responsibility gives them a sense of security and being loved. Of all the Energy States, you are certainly the most proactive. Because you are good at (and enjoy) solving problems and planning ahead, you naturally visualize problems before they arise and figure out how to avoid them. But your P focus may be too strong—you can get so caught up in the task at hand that you are unaware of or may even disregard the feelings of those around you, or you overlook a family situation that needs your immediate attention, in favor of some interesting professional problem. And if your P Energy State becomes aggravated by overheating, delayed meals, spicy foods, or someone challenging your authority, the extra heat will probably set off explosions.

Of all the types, Ps most need to keep their cool. Do not allow yourself to get hungry or thirsty. You can see that these things aggravate your P child, and of course, they do the same to you. Plan outdoor summer activities in the cool of the morning or evening. If your child's T-ball game or tennis match is at noon, wear a hat, try for a seat in the shade, and keep your bottle of cool water handy. Ice cream or a milkshake afterward is not only a treat but will help cool you down. P Energy State aromatherapy, especially at night, can help. If you think that you might have to deal with a potential confrontation—negotiating with your teenager about prom night, for example—plan to do it only after a good meal when everyone is fed and rested. Offer cool drinks.

## The K or Kapha Parent

As a K Energy State parent, you provide stability, strength, and loving comfort in your children's life. You are the bedrock, the foundation of their world. With your calm steadiness, you can structure and maintain a stable routine that provides a secure framework for their growth. And your stamina helps you ride out the ups and downs of parenting. But if you go beyond your limits of endurance, fatigue can drag that steadiness down into inertia, and your wonderful calmness can degrade to passivity and emotional withdrawal. It is important for you to carve some "off duty" time into your schedule in order for you to regroup and relax. While you would rather opt for watching your favorite movie, remember that K types are usually happier and more nourished when making or moving. Useful projects requiring painstaking work, or crafts such as woodworking or sewing will satisfy you more than passive entertainment.

K Energy State people have a tendency to become sedentary, so make it a point to keep yourself enlivened. Exercise is very important to keep your sturdy physiology from becoming sluggish and overweight. And if you can exercise as a group activity, that can be more ideal for you. It doesn't have to be aerobics or calisthenics—a wild game of tag, a brisk walk, or shooting hoops can get your family involved. Lighter foods—think fruit instead of cake, tortilla chips and popcorn instead of fries—will also help. And you are the one Energy State who does well with tasty spicy food! Remember that even though K Energy people are hard to get started, they are much more balanced and therefore happier, when they finally get moving. Do whatever you have to do ("trick" yourself if necessary) to start an exercise program (or that upholstery project you've been thinking about)—it will help keep your K Energy State in good balance and that will allow you to be a better parent.

## Agile and Parenting

I have some personal experience bringing Agile and Scrum into my family life, but first, let me refresh your memory about Scrum. The following are a few simple definitions that apply to software development:

• Scrum: a learning framework or set of practices in the Agile system of management used to improve teamwork in the creation of software

- Scrum Master: a coach who helps to improve a Scrum team's performance

- Product Manager: a member of a Scrum team who represents the stakeholder

- Stakeholder: represents the customer or department for whom the team is creating products

- Scrum Sprint: a repeatable or iterative work cycle (e.g. 1 or 2 weeks) during which an incremental part of the software product is completed

The following are excerpts from my blog on Iloveagilelife.com.

### Explaining Scrum to my 7 year-old son, Kyran

As my son and I are driving in the car, I make up a joke about Scrum.

"Why can't vampires be product owners?" I ask....

Pause. "Because they don't like to meet with stakeholders!"

His blank face tells me he doesn't get it. But he wants to. He even laughs.

Then he asks, "What is a product owner? Who are stakeholders?"

I start to explain Scrum. "It's a learning framework for creating software."

Another blank stare.

"It's a learning framework," I repeat, "with a team, a product owner, and a Scrum Master."

"That's you!" my son chimes graciously.

You can see how the conversation is going. I do my best to explain but I don't think much is understood. It gets me to thinking. How can I describe Scrum to him simply? For me, the heart of Agile and Scrum is teamwork. And if it really does rely on fundamental principles, it should be found in nature.

I think about Scrum qualities in nature. When we get home, I show him three images. The first is a picture of geese flying.

"When geese fly together," I tell him, "the body of each individual goose reduces air resistance for the goose flying behind it and the movement of their wings provides additional lift. Scientists estimate that by flying together in a V-formation the flock can fly about 70% farther using the same amount of energy that it would take for each goose to fly the same distance alone."

"Cool. I can see how working together helps each of the geese," he says.

Then I show him a photo of a large group of Emperor penguins huddled together. I explain, "Emperor penguins know the value of teamwork. Their lives and the lives of their young depend on it."

He gets that too.

I give him an image of one panda pushing another up onto a platform, and say, "One panda is helping the other achieve what it can't do on its own."

He seems to get why teamwork is important.

The next picture I show him is the image of a cross section of a tree trunk—a great example of how nature uses incremental and iterative processes to create amazing things.

"Each one of those rings is a year of the tree's life," I tell him. "By incrementally adding a ring each year trees can grow into amazing sizes and shapes."

"Like the big one in our yard," he says.

"Yeah, like that tree. It started out as a tiny seed and grew into something huge."

Then I show him a picture of a Nautilus shell, which is cut in half. "This shell forms one compartment, then the next, and the next. Nature creates in an ever increasing or incremental way, and it does this through repeated or iterative cycles."

Kyran nods knowingly.

So I show him images which represent communication. To me, communication is key to Scrum. First, I show him a picture of a widely smiling baby, and I ask him how he thinks the baby is feeling.

"Happy!"

"And this one?" Now I show him a picture of a baby crying angrily.

"Unhappy!" he says.

"If we can see someone and talk to them," I tell him, "it is much easier for us to understand how they are feeling."

He gets it.

"So," I continue, "I help to improve or facilitate teamwork and communication, and I use an iterative or repetitive as well as an incremental or ever-increasing process to create amazing things!"

After this, all he wanted to hear were more jokes.


**Two years later: Family Agile, the first week**

A month before Kyran's 9th birthday it occurs to me to use Scrum as a family improvement tool. Families have to solve complex problems all the time and Scrum is all about teamwork and communication.

Scrum uses Sprints or short intensive time periods to bring a project to completion and we created our own version of a family

Sprint, starting with a planning meeting. Kyran and one of his two sisters, Jace (age10), and my wife Danielle and I, used push pins to fasten a large sheet of paper to a cork board on the wall and placed lots of pens and sticky pads on the table. We then decided to establish the following rules or "code of conduct":

- Write your ideas on sticky notes and paste them on the board

- No adults kissing during the meeting (kid's suggestion)

- No grumpy or judgment faces (parent's suggestion)

- Full participation (parent's suggestion)

Our first meeting continued for 2-3 hours (amazing for kids 9 and 10) and the board was covered with lots of sticky notes. After talking about what we wanted to do as a family, we decided on an adventure, inspired by Kyran's upcoming birthday.

Kyran wanted to fly. Specifically, he wanted to do indoor skydiving. This was a big goal because we would have to drive 4 ½ hours to Chicago and it was expensive. At first we didn't think that we could do it, then we decided to wait until after Christmas. Finally, we just went for it. An additional goal was to create a movie of our adventure and put it on YouTube!

At the end of the meeting, all of us were tired but we were energized as a team. That was our biggest win—we were a team with a unified vision. Kyran came up with our rallying call, "Let's be an absolutely epic, amazing, awesome, family!"

Here is a link to our video—https://www.iloveagilelife.com/ single-post/2016/11/05/Family-Agile-the-First-Week

# CHAPTER 15

## LIFE COACHING

TBC life coaches use coaching skills from many different areas: health, relationships, career, and parenting. TBC life coaching is focused on helping your clients create good habits so they can fulfill their goals.

Again, it is important to understand that TBC does not involve any kind of therapy or counseling. We don't deal with the past. You have to help the client to assume full responsibility for themselves, focusing on their current reality and how to move forward to live their best possible lives. TBC is for people with problems as well as for those who are competent and successful. The job of the TBC coach is to listen carefully, and then carefully help the client to reach his or her own solution by creating new and more positive habits. Ultimately, TBC life coaching is about giving your client the ability to coach themselves so that they are empowered on their journey through the many challenges of life.

TBC life coaching helps to clarify your clients' vision of their future. Where do they want to be in 10 or 20 years? What is their priority in life—career, family, fame, money, or spirituality? What is holding them back? Are old habits limiting their behavior? Developing a profound and lasting trust with your clients will help develop an understanding of the core values that are motivating them.

In each case, you will work with your clients to create new habits that will help to maintain their Energy State in good balance so they can fulfill their desires in a way which benefits themselves and their loved ones. Each new challenge may require a unique set of TBC tools to help them move forward. As we have frequently mentioned, they need a habit plan, as well as clear, measurable objectives. Remember that it's important to break down the process of adopting a new habit into manageable steps. If there are obstacles in the client's environment, help them create a strategy to deal with them. Talk with them about what resources may be available to help fulfill their goals. With each step of progress, find ways to evaluate and celebrate your clients' success.

# ABOUT THE AUTHORS

Ted Wallace is currently an Agile Coach at Cambridge Investment Research, Inc. He has completed two Master of Science degrees, one in Computer Science and another in Physiology from Maharishi International University. He is also a certified Scrum Master Professional (CSM, CSPO, CSP) and a registered corporate coach (RCC) with thousands of hours of coaching sessions completed. See Forward for further details.

Dr. Robert Keith Wallace did pioneering research on the Transcendental Meditation technique. His seminal papers—published in *Science, American Journal of Physiology*, and *Scientific American*—on a fourth major state of consciousness supported a new paradigm of mind-body medicine and total brain development. Dr. Wallace is the founding President of Maharishi International University and has traveled around the world giving lectures at major universities and institutes on Consciousness-Based health programs. He is currently a Trustee of Maharishi International University, and Chairman of the Department of Physiology and Health.

Dr. Wallace has written and co-authored a number of books, the latest of which is *The Rest And Repair Diet: Heal Your Gut,*

*Improve Your Physical and Mental Health, and Lose Weight.*

A former model, Samantha Wallace was featured on the covers of *Vogue, Cosmopolitan,* and *Look* magazines. She is a long-time practitioner of Transcendental Meditation, and has a deep understanding of Ayurveda and its relationship to health and well being. Samantha co-authored *Gut Crisis* and *The Rest And Repair Diet,* which integrate ancient Ayurvedic wisdom with the latest findings in modern medicine.

She is also the co-author of *Quantum Golf,* and was an editor of *Dharma Parenting.* Her most recent book is *Beauty And Being Yourself: A User-Friendly Introduction to Ayurveda And Essential Oil Skincare,* co-authored by Dr. Wallace and Veronica Wells Butler, M.D.

Happily married for over forty years, the Wallaces have a combined family of four children and six grandchildren.

# ACKNOWLEDGMENTS

We would like to thank Fran Clark and Rick Nakata for proofreading.

# Part 4

## Resource Material

Some of the following material also appears in *The Coherence Code* by Robert Keith Wallace, PhD, Ted Wallace, MS, Samantha Wallace.

# 1

# Energy States And Ayurveda

Ayurveda is a comprehensive, prevention-oriented system of natural medicine that addresses our body, mind, and environment. In this holistic approach to health, each person is evaluated according to his or her individual mind/body type or nature. Traditionally, the three basic Energy States have been called Vata, Pitta, and Kapha doshas. As much as possible, we abbreviate these words to V for Vata, P for Pitta, and K for Kapha: V, P, and K.

In each of our books we have used a slightly different term to refer to the doshas. In *Gut Crisis* and *The Rest And Repair Diet* we use the term Gut/Brain Nature in order to emphasize the importance of the gut-brain axis to your health. In Dharma Parenting we use the brain/body type.

Your Energy State can be determined either by answering a simple questionnaire, or by an examination by a trained Ayurveda expert. Scientific research demonstrates that the Energy State is correlated with individual genetic and physiological measures, and with the composition of the gut bacteria (see Resource Material 2 for more details).

## The 3 Main Energy States

### V Energy State

V Energy State individuals are bright, good at creating new ideas and projects, and able to learn quickly. If, however, they become imbalanced, they easily lose their energy and can become fatigued and oversensitive. They may also experience mood swings, and they will then have difficulty in following a project through to the end. The secret for a V person to maintain balance is to follow a good routine. Certain simple dietary and lifestyle changes will also greatly help to rebalance and sustain the energy of a V individual.

The following charts are adapted from *Dharma Parenting*.

## IMBALANCE IN THE V ENERGY STATE

### Causes of V Imbalance

| | |
|---|---|
| Overstimulation | Too many choices |
| Overexertion | Negative emotions |
| Irregular routine | Stressful situations |
| Cold and/or windy weather | Unpleasant interactions with others |
| Excessive travel | |

### Signs of V Imbalance

| | |
|---|---|
| Hyperactivity | Restless |
| Easily distracted | High strung |
| Overly emotional | Forgetful |
| Anxious | Poor digestion |
| Nervous | Constipation |
| Fearful | Irregular appetite |
| Lonely | Spacey |
| Quickly changing moods | |

### Recommendations To Balance V Energy State

| | |
|---|---|
| Establish and maintain a daily routine | Take extra rest to recharge |
| Avoid cold, windy weather | Have healthy and delicious snacks |
| Reduce excessive stimulations | Create a bedtime routine |
| Guard against fatigue | Enjoy creative activities |
| Focus on specific goals | |

## P Energy State

P Energy State individuals have a great deal of energy and staying power. They can also be very aggressive, and often possess a strong and penetrating intellect. They tend to be well-organized and can be good decision-makers. It is no coincidence that businesspeople and athletes are frequently P individuals. When a P is imbalanced, they may have trouble controlling their anger, or, at the very least, irritation, from time to time. They can also be impatient, difficult to interact with, and controlling. The key to keeping a P in good balance is to eat on time and not get overheated. (It's that simple!)

| IMBALANCE IN THE P ENERGY STATE | |
|---|---|
| **Causes of P Imbalance** | |
| Overheating<br><br>Not eating on time<br><br>Not drinking enough water<br><br>Negative emotions | Overly competitive or aggressive situations<br><br>Hot spices such as chilies |
| **Signs of P Imbalance** | |
| Irritable<br><br>Angry<br><br>Impatient<br><br>Critical<br><br>Jealous<br><br>Hostile<br><br>Obsessive-compulsive behaviors | Intense hunger<br><br>Excessive thirst<br><br>Sensitivity to spicy and/or fried foods, with indigestion and/or heartburn<br><br>Excessive sweating<br><br>Temper tantrums |
| **Recommendations To Balance P Energy State** | |
| Eat on time, especially at lunch<br><br>Prevent overheating<br><br>Keep well-hydrated<br><br>Avoid foods with "hot" spices | Enjoy physical activity during the day<br><br>On hot days turn on air conditioning<br><br>On mild days keep the windows open |

**K Energy State**

K Energy State people tend to be steady and take some time to carefully consider any decision. They are not easily upset, and are often easygoing and agreeable. If they go out of balance, however, they can become stubborn and lack ambition. The key to keeping a K person in good balance is to keep them physically active and mentally stimulated.

| IMBALANCE IN THE K ENERGY STATE | |
|---|---|
| **Causes of K Imbalance** | |
| Too little activity | Exposure to excessively hot, humid weather |
| Lack of mental stimulation | |
| Lack of regular exercise | Exposure to cold, damp weather |
| Overeating | Excessive sleep |
| **Signs of K Imbalance** | |
| Stubborn | Sad |
| Depressed | Withdrawn |
| Lethargic | Excess mucus |
| Lazy | Weight gain |
| **Recommendations To Balance K Energy State** | |
| Keep mentally and physically stimulated | Try not to overeat: light meals are best |
| Include regular outdoor activity and exercise | Allow extra time for everything |

## Energy State Combinations

## VP (PV) Energy States

A VP Energy State person is similar to someone who has a PV Energy State, but it is important to note that whichever Energy State is listed first will tend to dominate. A VP person is quick, inspiring, and full of new ideas, but at the same time focused and ready to complete the project. VPs can be both energetic and sensitive. One side of them is in motion, while the other is goal-oriented.

When VPs are in good balance, they draw energy from their P qualities. When they are out of balance, their V qualities can cause them to become over-stimulated and quickly exhausted. This duality produces a reasonably strong but variable energy.

### VP Digestion

The digestion of a VP is like their energy, strong but variable, and their appetite is good. Because their gut is partially V, they may be a picky or discriminating eater with strong preferences, and can be hungry one minute and not the next. Because their gut is also partially P, they need ample meals to sustain physical and mental activity. The presence of P indicates that it is especially important for VP individuals to eat on time. As a combination type, they have a more balanced appetite than people with a pure V or pure P Energy State.

When VPs are in good balance, they rarely have digestive problems. When out of balance, however, digestive issues can range from weak digestion to hyperactivity.

**VP Exercise**

VP Energy State people are agile and graceful and have good energy and strength.

**VP Sleep**

VP Energy individuals do not have a problem falling asleep unless they get over-stimulated right before going to bed.

## VK (KV) Energy State

This Energy State is an interesting combination of opposites. The V Energy State is light and airy, while the K Energy State is heavy and earthy. This combination of states indicates both steadiness and enthusiasm.

When VK is in good balance, the result is good health and physical stamina. When it is out of balance, VK people are prone to frequent colds and respiratory problems. With this particular energy state, it's important to remember that an imbalance of V will always push K out of balance, so V imbalances need to be addressed as soon as possible. VKs don't do well in cold or damp weather, and to avoid illness need to stay warm.

The VK combination gives rise to individuals who have a wide range of emotions. VKs are quick, inspiring, and full of new ideas, but at the same time they are stable, well liked, and methodical. VKs can be both grounded and sensitive. One part of them is in motion, while the other is steady and constant.

When out of balance, a VK person tends to be spacey, withdrawn, or even depressed. They may also obsess on issues, and become attached and/or anxious. It's especially good for VKs to have enjoyable social outings and stay rested, energized, and happy, in order to improve every aspect of their mind, body, and emotions.

**VK Digestion**

The digestion of a VK Energy State person (virtually the same as a KV Energy State person except that whichever energy state is listed first predominates), is generally strong and steady, and they enjoy an occasional snack. The V part of the VK combination makes the person a grazer with a constantly changing appetite, while the K part makes them love to eat. V and K complement each other when they are in balance. So, they enjoy food, but don't gain as much weight as pure K types.

When out of balance, their digestion slows down and they become more sensitive to what they eat.

**VK Exercise**

VK Energy State individuals have a mixture of opposite tendencies and can be both a sprinter and an endurance runner.

**VK Sleep**

VK Energy individuals can fall asleep and stay asleep as long their V Energy State is balanced.

## PK (KP) Energy State

PK Energy State people have the hot, transformative qualities of a P Energy State plus the cool, stable qualities of a K Energy State. But if they don't stay in balance, they can boil over. PKs are generally large and strong. They might not be the star of the team, but they have the constitution to be a very good player.

A PK tends to be strong, sturdy, content, and easygoing. Their drive is steadied by their calm, easygoing nature. However, imbalances can cause impatience, anger, and lethargy. They can also become argumentative, stubborn, and withdrawn. It's very important for a PK, particularly, to maintain healthy family relationships and friendships in order to stay in good balance.

In the heat of the moment a PK might not think problems through completely. And if decisions backfire, they may be prone to useless regret. A PK individual will be happier and healthier if he or she spends more time listening and less time making assumptions and running scenarios in their head.

### PK Digestion

The digestion and appetite of a PK Energy State person (which is virtually the same as KP, only P will predominate) are both strong. Anyone with a P gut has a good appetite. With a PK gut, they will have an even stronger appetite. PKs like to eat and can generally digest easily. However, because their gut is part K, their metabolism can slow down at times and they can have a hard time digesting greasy foods. Although it's easy for PKs to gain a few extra pounds, they can usually lose them without great effort.

When PKs are in good balance, they rarely have digestive problems. When out of balance, however, they must be aware of slower digestion and hyperacidity.

**PK Exercise**

PKs need to exercise daily. PKs have excellent stamina in activity, but have to be careful not to get overheated.

**PK Sleep**

The PK or KP individual generally falls asleep easily and gets a good sound sleep.

## VPK Energy State or "Tri-Energy State"

This is a relatively rare mixture of the three types, and when in balance, it shows the best qualities of each. VPKs are often creative, motivated, steady, and good-natured. When they are in good balance, they tend to be in tune with their body and emotions, and can be intuitive. Physically strong with a moderate build, VPKs are usually in good health. They avoid most seasonal illnesses and experience only mild to moderate symptoms during each season (e.g. dry skin in the winter, some lethargy in the spring, and mild heat intolerance in the summer).

Life becomes complicated when one or more of their three Energy States goes out of balance. Often it is not clear which Energy State is first to go out of balance. Learn to "check in with yourself" and be alert to when something doesn't feel quite right. The best advice for VPKs is to treat imbalances in the following order: 1) Start with balancing V; 2) Go on to balance P; 3) Finally, address K. Keep in mind that it takes a VPK Energy State longer to come back into balance than other combinations of Energy States.

## VPK Digestion

The digestion and appetite of a VPK Energy State person should be good. Since they have a stronger digestion than others, they can eat almost any kind of food and rarely experience excessive hunger or thirst. But because their symptoms are usually mild and somewhat veiled, it's hard to pinpoint how and when they go out of balance, so it's especially valuable for them to learn to listen to their body.

## VPK Exercise

Since VPKs possess all three characteristics, any exercise is possible. The main thing is not to overdo it.

## VPK Sleep

Because this is a part K Energy State, sleep is their friend. If they do go out of balance, it is usually the V Energy State, which might cause them sleep problems.

**Conclusion**

No single Energy State is better than another and each of us can rise to our full potential by staying in balance and achieving maximum levels of energy, performance, and success.

For recommendations about specific Energy State diets, teas, spice mixes, and recipes, see *The Rest and Repair Diet: Heal Your Gut, Improve Your Physical and Mental Health, and Lose Weight,* and visit our website at docgut.com.

2

# Scientific Research on Ayurveda Energy States

Recent studies have shown that there is a scientific basis to Ayurveda and its evaluation of each person's Energy State or Prakriti.

Genetic research, for example, has shown that the V (Vata), P (Pitta), and K (Kapha) Energy State or Prakriti each express a different set of genes (1, 2). Genes in the immune response pathways, for example, were turned on (up-regulated) in the extreme Pittas. Genes related to cell cycles were turned on in Vatas, and genes in the immune signaling pathways were turned on in Kaphas. Inflammatory genes were up-regulated in Vatas, whereas up-regulation of oxidative stress pathway genes were observed in Pittas and Kaphas (3). CD25 (activated B cells) and CD56 (natural killer cells) were higher in Kaphas. CYP2C19 genotypes, a family of genes that help in detoxification and metabolism of certain drugs were turned off (down-regulated) in Kapha types and turned on in Pitta types (4, 5).

Extreme Vata, Pitta, and Kapha individuals also have significant differences in specific physiological measurements (1, 2). Triglycerides, total cholesterol, high low-density lipoprotein (LDL), and low high-DL (HDL) concentrations—all common risk factors for cardiovascular disease—were reported to be higher in Kaphas (K Energy State individuals) compared to Pittas (P Energy State individuals) and Vatas (V Energy State individuals). Hemoglobin and red blood count were higher in Pittas compared to others. Serum prolactin was higher in Vata individuals (2). High levels of triglyceride, VLDL and LDL levels and lower levels of HDL cholesterol distinguish Kaphas from others (6).

Adenosine diphosphate-induced maximal platelet aggregation was the highest among Vata/Pitta types (7). In diabetic patients, there were significant decreases in systolic blood pressure in Vata/ Pitta, Pitta/Kapha, and Vata/Kapha types after walking (isotonic exercise). The Vata/Pitta types also showed significant decreases in mean diastolic blood pressure (8). In terms of biochemistry, Kaphas had elevated digoxin levels, increased free radical production and reduced scavenging, increased tryptophan catabolites and reduced tyrosine catabolites, increased glycoconjugate levels, and increased cholesterol. Pittas showed the opposite biochemical patterns. Vatas showed normal biochemical patterns (9).

A study of basic cardiovascular responses reported that heart rate variability and arterial blood pressure during specific postural changes, exercise, and cold pressor test did not vary with constitutional type (10). A more recent paper measuring cold pressor test, standing-to-lying ratio, and pupillary responses in light and dark reported that Kapha types have higher parasympathetic activity and lower sympathetic activity in terms of cardiovascular reactivity as compared to Pitta or Vata types (11).

A recent study published in Frontiers in Microbiology also

showed that predominantly Vata, Pitta, or Kapha people also show a different composition of bacteria in their microbiome (12). Finally, Travis and Wallace have reviewed many of these findings, and created a neurophysiological model of Vata, Pitta, or Kapha based on the functioning of different neural networks (13).

## References

1. Dey S, Pahwa P. Prakriti and its associations with metabolism, chronic diseases, and genotypes: Possibilities of new born screening and a lifetime of personalized prevention. *J Ayurveda Integr Med* 2014;5:15-24.

2. Prasher B, Negi S, Aggarwal S, Mandal AK, Sethi TP, Deshmukh SR, et al. Whole genome expression and biochemical correlates of extreme constitutional types defined in Ayurveda. *J Transl Med* 2008;6:48.

3. Juyal RC, Negi S, Wakhode P, Bhat S, Bhat B, Thelma BK. Potential of ayurgenomics approach in complex trait research: Leads from a pilot study on rheumatoid arthritis. *PLoS One.* 2012;7:e45752.

4. Ghodke Y, Joshi K, Patwardhan B. Traditional medicine to modern pharmacogenomics: Ayurveda Prakriti type and CYP2C19 gene polymorphism associated with the metabolic variability. Evid Based *Complement Alternat Med* 2011;2011:249528.

5. Aggarwal S, Negi S, Jha P, Singh PK, Stobdan T, Pasha MA. Indian genome variation consortium. EGLN1 involvement in high-altitude adaptation revealed through genetic analysis of

extreme constitution types defined in Ayurveda. *Proc Natl Acad Sci* 2010;107:18961-6.

6. Mahalle NP, Kulkarni MV, Pendse NM, Naik SS. Association of constitutional type of Ayurveda with cardiovascular risk factors, inflammatory markers and insulin resistance. *J Ayurveda Integr Med* 2012;3:150-7.

7. Bhalerao S, Deshpande T, Thatte U. Prakriti (Ayurvedic concept of constitution) and variations in Platelet aggregation. BMC *Complement Altern Med* 2012;12:248-56.

8. Tiwari S, Gehlot S, Tiwari SK, Singh G. Effect of walking (aerobic isotonic exercise) on physiological variants with special reference to Prameha (diabetes mellitus) as per Prakriti. *Ayu* 2012;33:44-9.

9. Kurup RK, Kurup PA. Hypothalamic digoxin, hemispheric chemical dominance, and the tridosha theory. *Int J Neurosci* 2003;113:657-81.

10. Tripathi PK, Patwardhan K, Singh G. The basic cardiovascular responses to postural changes, exercise and cold pressor test: Do they vary in accordance with the dual constitutional types of Ayurveda? *Evid Based Complement Alternat Med* 2011;201:251-9.

11. Rapolu SB, Kumar M, Singh G, Patwardhan K. Physiological variations in the autonomic responses may be related to the constitutional types defined in Ayurveda. *J Humanitas Med* 2015;5:e7.

12. Chauhan NS, Pandey R, Mondal AK, Gupta S, Verma MK, Jain S, et al. Western Indian Rural Gut Microbial Diversity in Extreme Prakriti Endo-Phenotypes Reveals Signature Microbes. *Front. Microbiol.* 2018; 9:118. doi: 10.3389/fmicb.2018.00118.

eCollection 2018.

13. Travis, FT, Wallace, RK, Dosha brain-types: A neural model of individual differences. *J Ayurveda Integr Med*. 2015; 6, 280-85.

3

# Recommendations

## Meditation

Everybody knows that meditation helps people deal with stress, but which kind of meditation is best for you? Recent research clearly shows that different types of meditation are not the same. There are three main categories of meditation procedure, each with different effects on the brain:

- Focused Attention (including Zen, compassion, qigong, and vipassana): gamma (fast) EEG indicates that the brain is concentrated and focused.

- Open Monitoring (including mindfulness and Kriya yoga): theta (slow) EEG indicates that the mind is in a more contemplative state, following its own internal mental processes.

- Automatic self-transcending (including Transcendental Meditation): coherent alpha1 (foundational) EEG indicates that the mind is in a unique state of restful alertness.

The first two types of meditation construct mental tools to help us cope with life. Generally speaking, Focused Attention meditations train the mind to concentrate more closely and for longer periods. Open Monitoring meditations, which include many techniques of mindfulness, help us develop greater awareness of our body (such as our breathing patterns), and cultivate insight into what we are thinking and doing.

Automatic Self-Transcending meditations are fundamentally different because they do not involve thinking about something—rather, they allow the mind to settle down to a very quiet state while becoming more alert. The goal of Transcendental Meditation is not to develop a specific mental ability, such as improved concentration, but rather to improve the mind's basic functioning by making it more settled and alert. The word "transcend" means to go beyond, and when we transcend during TM we go beyond thoughts and categories—we are, in effect, stepping outside the boundaries of our problems. After our TM practice, we come back to our situation better able to see the big picture and find creative solutions.

Because we have personally experienced—and, in the case of Dr. R.K. Wallace, as a researcher—how effective Transcendental Meditation is, Total Brain Coaching focuses on the Transcendental Meditation technique. (See TM.org for more details on TM.)

## Yoga

Yoga has long been recognized as a method to improve and maintain your body while you are on the path to health, happiness, success, fulfillment, and, ultimately, enlightenment. Research shows that yoga postures or asanas improve certain psychological conditions, including anxiety and depression, and provide health benefits for those with high blood pressure, various pain syndromes, and immune disorders.

Choose whichever form of yoga best suits your individual Energy State, age, and needs. We recommend the Maharishi Yoga Asana program because it is especially respectful of your body and your consciousness, and supports the experience of transcendence.

## Beauty

Former model Samantha Wallace, Robert Keith Wallace, PhD, Veronica Butler, MD, have written *Beauty And Being Yourself: A User-Friendly Introduction to Ayurveda And Essential Oil Skincare*. *Beauty And Being Yourself* includes a quiz to determine your True Skin Type and explains how understanding your True Skin Type gives you an extraordinary guide to caring for your skin, your health, and your inner and outer beauty at any age.

After reading this book, you can look at the label of any skin product and be able to answer the following:

- Does it contain oils that are good for my particular skin?

- Are the Essential Oils listed worth the price?

- Are there any chemicals I should check for toxicity?

## The Gut-Brain Connection

One of the most important achievements of modern science is the discovery of the gut-brain connection. This complex network called the gut-brain axis has an enormous impact on the health of your body and mind. The gut-brain axis consists of a number of major physiological systems: the nervous system, enteric nervous system or ENS, endocrine system, immune system, and the gut bacteria or microbiome.

The microbiome is technically defined as all of the microorganisms that live in you or on you—including their genetic material. The vast majority of these microorganisms, however, are the 30 trillion friendly bacteria that live in your lower gut.

We used to believe that all bacteria were harmful. And while it's true that certain virulent bacteria and viruses are capable of killing millions of people, it turns out that most of the bacteria living in your gut are wonderfully beneficial. There is a two-way communication between the gut and the brain. Stress in your brain can disrupt your digestive process, while stress in your gut can disrupt your mind and emotions.

Gut bacteria use the vagus nerve to communicate with your brain, and also produce a wide variety of chemical messengers, including neurotransmitters and hormones that can enter the bloodstream and affect parts of your brain. Brain imaging has shown that people react differently to stress, depending on the type of bacteria in their gut. Subjects receiving a probiotic showed a reduced stress response, with less activity in the emotional areas of the brain.

By understanding the connection between the brain and the gut, we can better understand the basic principles of ancient systems of health such as Ayurveda. These natural systems of health place a great emphasis on improving digestion and removing toxins from the body.

Hippocrates, considered to be the father of Western medicine, said, "All disease begins in the gut." In the past, doctors used to consider this a strange concept, but now most doctors and scientists understand that your gut bacteria have an enormous impact on both your mind and body, and that they may be key to the treatment of many disorders and diseases—from diabetes to Alzheimer's, even obesity. The state of your health depends upon the state of your digestion and gut bacteria.

The problem is that many people have adopted bad habits, which disrupt the gut and can eventually lead to chronic disease. Your gut needs a chance to rest and repair itself and to re-enliven your own inner intelligence. This may sound simplistic, but it works. Rest enables your body's repair systems to kick in and begin to heal and re-establish balance in your gut. Fatigue is the enemy.

To improve the health of the gut we have developed a specific diet, which combines the ancient knowledge of Ayurveda with the latest findings of modern medicine. This diet is called *The Rest and Repair Diet*, and in addition to improving digestion and gut bacteria it also helps to promote clearer awareness so that you can make other positive changes in your lifestyle and activities.

For more details on this program see *The Rest And Repair Diet*:

*Heal Your Gut, Improve Your Physical and Mental Health, and Lose Weight* by Robert Keith Wallace, PhD, Samantha Wallace, Andrew Stenberg, MA, Jim Davis, DO, and Alexis Farley, Dharma Publications, 2019.

For more information on the microbiome and gut bacteria see *Gut Crisis: How Diet, Probiotics, and Friendly Bacteria Help You Lose Weight and Heal Your Body and Mind* by Robert Keith Wallace, PhD, and Samantha Wallace, Dharma Publications, 2017.

4

# Self Pulse

An effective tool to use in Total Brain Self-Coaching is self pulse diagnosis as taught in Maharishi AyurVeda. Because your cardiovascular system extends throughout your body—from your eyeballs to your liver to the joints of your big toe—it carries a wealth of information about how your physiology is functioning. Ayurvedic physicians are trained to "read" and decode this information by simply touching your wrist with three fingers. In this way they can assess balance and imbalance, and even detect disease. You can learn a simplified method of self pulse diagnosis to keep track of your state of balance or imbalance.

**Let's start with some definitions:**

Wrist: It's very important to note that women always feel the pulse that beats in their left wrist, while men always feel the pulse in the right wrist. So in these instructions, wrist refers to a woman's left wrist or a man's right wrist.

Fingers: A woman uses the fingertips of her right hand to feel her left wrist; a man uses the fingertips of his left hand. So fingers and hand refer to a woman's right hand, or a man's left hand.

Styloid process: This boney projection is about a finger's width below the base of your thumb—use your index finger to feel it sticking out. This is the reference point for figuring out where to place your fingers.

**Taking the Pulse**

To take your pulse, extend your arm out in front of you—right arm for men, left for women—in a comfortable position, slightly bent at the elbow, with your palm facing up. Now wrap your other hand around your wrist from behind. You are cradling the back of your wrist in the palm of your other hand. Now curl the middle three fingers—index, middle, and ring fingers—over the top of your wrist.

Position your index finger below the prominent bony bump of the styloid process, so that it's just beside the edge of this bone.

Now line up your middle and ring fingers below your index finger so the three are touching each other easily side by side. And make sure the three fingers are completely level; raise your thumb and little finger slightly so they're not touching your wrist. This is the position your fingers will always be in when you take your pulse.

Continue to slide your three fingers over and down your wrist about a quarter of an inch. Now you are ready to feel your pulse: using your fingertips very gently press all three fingers down until you can feel the pulse beating along the radial artery. It's important to use all three fingers together and make sure that your three fingertips are approximately level, sitting in a nice line at the same level of the pulse. When you can feel the beat of your pulse in any one, or all, of your fingertips, you will have reached the first stage of pulse reading.

Each of your three fingers corresponds to one of the three main Energy States: the index finger for V Energy State or Vata; the middle finger for P Energy State or Pitta; the ring finger for K Energy State or Kapha. (Kapha may be so relaxed, or there may be so little Kapha, that it might be hard to feel it at all.)

Feel the pulse beneath each finger. (It can help to close your eyes.) Which finger feels the strongest pulse? For example, if you feel it strongest under your middle finger, that indicates that the P Energy State is strong.

You may or may not feel a pulsation beneath all three fingertips—this is perfectly normal. In fact, most people feel their pulse under one or two fingers; only a few feel it under all three. If you're predominately a V Energy State person, for example, the pulse under your index finger will be strong. You may feel little or nothing under the other two fingers. This doesn't necessarily mean that you're imbalanced—it does means that at this time, your physiology has less Pitta fire or Kapha solidity in it.

What is the quality of your pulse? If it feels clear and the impulses seem coordinated—if it feels good to you overall—this indicates that your physiology is in good balance. If your pulse feels ragged or disconnected, with some impulses very weak while another is very pronounced, this tells you that you probably want to start getting yourself back in balance.

As an example, you may feel that P Energy State area is pulsating very strongly under your index finger, which indicates that your P Energy State or Pitta is too strong and has invaded V's territory. It's time to stay cool and eat on time — but not at your favorite Mexican restaurant. If the pulse under your ring finger feels quick and irregular, you need to get your V Energy State in better balance. Slow down, stay out of the cold wind, and stick to a regular routine. If your K Energy State or Kapha feels very strong and dense under your middle finger, you may find that your digestion is sluggish and your mind is a bit dull. Balance that aggravated K Energy State with some physical activity and fewer "heavy" foods such as desserts and mashed potatoes.

# 5

## Maharishi AyurVeda

Maharishi AyurVeda is a revival of Ayurveda, which includes consciousness-based approaches to health as well as an advanced methodology of pulse diagnosis. Maharishi International University (MIU) was founded by Maharishi Mahesh Yogi, who is also the founder of the Transcendental Meditation technique, and Maharishi AyurVeda. MIU offers an online Master of Science degree in Maharishi AyurVeda and Integrative Medicine. The program is a 3-year part-time online program, which integrates the ancient knowledge of Ayurveda with what has been discovered by modern medicine. It is taught by qualified doctors, and students are given in-residence clinical training by Maharishi AyurVeda experts for two weeks each year. MIU is a member of the National Ayurvedic Medical Association and is accredited by the Higher Learning Commission. MIU also offers an online and in-residence BA in Ayurveda Wellness and Integrative Health. See MIU.edu for more details.

# REFERENCES

## Websites And Books

### Useful Websites

Totalbraincoaching.com

TM.org

MIU.edu

### Useful Books

*The Coherence Code: How to Maximum Your Performance And Success in Business - For Individuals, Teams, and Organizations* by Robert Keith Wallace, PhD, Ted Wallace, MS, Samantha Wallace, Dharma Publications, 2020

*Atomic Habit: An Easy & Proven Way to Build Good Habits & Break Bad Ones* by James Clear, Avery, 2018

*Mindset: The New Psychology of Success* by Carol S. Dweck, Ballantine Books, 2007

*Triggers: Creating Behavior That Lasts—Becoming the Person You Want to Be* by Marshall Goldsmith and Mark Reiter, Crown Business, 2015

*The Power of Habit: Why We Do What We Do in Life and Business* by Charles Duhigg, Random House, 2012

*Hit Refresh: The Quest to Rediscover Microsoft's Soul and Imagine a Better Future for Everyone* by Satya Nadella, Greg Shaw, Jill Tracie Nichols, Harper Business, 2017

*Principles* by Ray Dalio, Simon & Schuster, 2017

*Evolvagility: Growing an Agile Leadership Culture from the Inside* by Michael Hamman, Agile Leadership Institute, 2019

*Coaching Agile Teams: A Companion for Scrum Masters, Agile Coaches, and Project Managers in Transition* by Lyssa Adkins, Addison-Wesley, 2010

*The Age of Agile: How Smart Companies Are Transforming the Way Work Gets Done* by Stephen Denning, Amacon, 2018

*The Progress Principle: Using Small Wins to Ignite Joy, Engagement, and Creativity at Work by Teresa M. Amabile and Steven J. Kramer, Harvard Business Review Press, 2011*

*Gut Crisis: How Diet, Probiotics, and Friendly Bacteria Help You Lose Weight and Heal Your Body and Mind* by Robert Keith Wallace, PhD, and Samantha Wallace, Dharma Publications, 2017

*The Rest And Repair Diet: Heal Your Gut, Improve Your Physical and Mental Health, and Lose Weight* by Robert Keith Wallace, PhD, Samantha Wallace, Andrew Stenberg, MA, Jim Davis, DO, and Alexis Farley, Dharma Publications, 2019

*Dharma Parenting: Understand Your Child's Brilliant Brain for Greater Happiness, Health, Success, and Fulfillment* by Robert Keith Wallace, PhD, and Fredrick Travis, PhD, Tarcher/Perigree, 2016

*Beauty And Being Yourself: A User-Friendly Introduction to Ayurveda And Essential Oil Skincare* by Samantha Wallace, Robert Keith Wallace, PhD, Veronica Butler, MD, Dharma Publications, 2020

*World-Class Brain* by Harald Harung, PhD and Frederick Travis, PhD, Harvest, AS, 2019

*Success from Within: Discovering the Inner State that Creates Personal Fulfillment and Business Success* by Jay B. Marcus, MUM Press, 1990

*Enlightened Management: Building High-Performance People* by Gerald Swanson and Bob Oates, MUM Press, 1987

*Science of Being and Art of Living: Transcendental Meditation* by Maharishi Mahesh Yogi, MUM Press, Kindle edition, 2011

*Maharishi's Absolute Theory of Government* by Maharishi Mahesh Yogi, MUM Press, 1995

*Maharishi Mahesh Yogi on the Bhagavad-Gita, A New Translation and Commentary, Chapters 1-6*, MUM Press, 2016

*Strength in Stillness: The Power of Transcendental Meditation* by Bob Roth, Simon & Schuster, 2018

*Catching the Big Fish: Meditation, Consciousness, and Creativity* by David Lynch, Tarcher/Penguin 2007

*An Introduction to Transcendental Meditation: Improve Your Brain Functioning, Create Ideal Health, and Gain Enlightenment Naturally, Easily, Effortlessly* by Robert Keith Wallace, PhD, and Lincoln Akin Norton, Dharma Publications, 2016

*Transcendental Meditation: A Scientist's Journey to Happiness, Health, and Peace*, Adapted and Updated from The Physiology of Consciousness: Part 1 by Robert Keith Wallace, PhD, Dharma Publications, 2016

*The Neurophysiology of Enlightenment: How the Transcendental Meditation and TM-Sidhi Program Transform the Functioning of the Human Body*, by Robert Keith Wallace, PhD, Dharma Publications, 2016

*Maharishi Ayurveda and Vedic Technology: Creating Ideal Health for the Individual and World*, Adapted and Updated from The Physiology of Consciousness: Part 2 by Robert Keith Wallace, PhD, Dharma Publications, 2016

*In Balance leben: Wie wir trotz Stress mit unserer Energie richtig umgehen Broschiert* (Translation: *Living in Balance: How to deal with our energy properly despite stress.*) by Dr. med. Ulrich Bauhofer, Südwest Verlag, 2013

*Quantum Golf: The Path to Golf Mastery* by Kjell Enhager and Samantha Wallace, Warner Books, New York, 1991

# Index

Habit Plan  vi, 10, 31, 74, 85
health coaching  14, 42, 93

## I

Inner Rhythm  vi, 7, 11

## K

K Energy State  19, 26, 32, 33, 46, 52, 54, 56, 57, 58, 97, 104, 105, 124, 125, 127, 129, 131, 134, 147, 148
Kolbe  17, 74

## L

leadership coach  89
life coaching  14, 111

## M

Maharishi AyurVeda  vii, 94, 145, 149
Maharishi International University  94, 113, 149
Maharishi Mahesh Yogi  149, 153
meditation  40, 41, 59, 96, 139
microbiome  41, 42, 135, 142, 144
Microsoft  152
mindset  1, 3, 14, 46, 49, 81, 82, 83, 87, 89
Myers-Briggs  17

## N

neural pruning  36
neuroplasticity  vi, 6, 10, 36

## P

parent coaching  14, 101, 102
P Energy State  19, 25, 31, 33, 38, 49, 50, 52, 55, 56, 58, 64, 85, 96, 97, 103, 122, 123, 126, 129, 134, 147, 148
Personal Coaching  8, 62, 76
Power of Attention  vi, 7, 11

## R

relationship coaching  14, 95
routines  54

CPSIA information can be obtained
at www.ICGtesting.com
Printed in the USA
FSHW010858110120
65989FS

9 780999 055878